Basketball

Basketball

Brian Naysmith & Terry Hill

DAVID & CHARLES
NEWTON ABBOT . LONDON
NORTH POMFRET (Vt) . VANCOUVER

British Library Cataloguing in Publication Data

Naysmith, Brian
  Basketball.
  1. Basketball
  I. Title II. Hill, Terry
  796.32'32   GV885

ISBN 0-7153-7509-1

Library of Congress Catalog Card Number 77-**91725**

© Brian Naysmith & Terry Hill 1978
All rights reserved. No part of this publication may be reproduced, stored in a retrieval system, or transmitted, in any form or by any means, electronic, mechanical, photocopying, recording or otherwise, without the prior permission of David & Charles (Publishers) Limited

Printed in Great Britain
by Redwood Burn Limited
for David & Charles (Publishers) Limited
Brunel House Newton Abbot Devon

Published in the United States of America
by David & Charles Inc
North Pomfret Vermont 05053 USA

Published in Canada
by Douglas David & Charles Limited
1875 Welch Street North Vancouver BC

Contents

INTRODUCTION		7
1	How to Start	9
2	The Rules	15
3	Individual Skills	28
4	Team Defence	52
5	Attack	63
6	Team Practice	70
7	Mini-Basketball	80
GLOSSARY		91
APPENDIX: Details of the Leagues and Cup Competitions within Britain; Names and Addresses of National League Clubs, Areas and Area Secretaries		101

Dedication

We would like to express our thanks to all those players from Southern Grammar School, Southern Eagles, Southern Pirates (Portsmouth), Manchester 'Y' and Stretford Basketball Club, without whom this book would not have been possible.

We would also like to thank Pam West for typing, re-typing, correcting and indexing the book, and Glen Ashley for the illustrations.

Introduction

In 1891 Dr James Naismith sought a new game which would eliminate unnecessary contact and where running with and kicking the ball would not be major skills. He wanted a game which would satisfy aesthetically, a game the purist or the artist could enjoy without being overcome physically and which had as major skills ball-handling (but not ball-hogging), speed and athleticism.

The result of his thoughts is the game of basketball, now administered by the Federation Internationale de Basketball Amateur (FIBA) which has 130 member nations controlling 80 million basketball players. In Britain there are 100,000 registered players and many more unregistered players and teams.

We know from statistics that it is the most popular game in the world, but figures do not in themselves provide a compelling reason to play it. That comes from the ingredients of the game itself: the individual skills of dribbling, passing, shooting and defending are exhilarating and, when combined with the team skills in offence and defence, then basketball can give satisfaction to the most demanding sportsperson.

Much development has taken place since the early days of basketball and changes have been made with the result that the game no longer completely conforms to the earlier ideals. For instance, no one would now claim that basketball is a non-contact game as there are many very big men playing whose physical presence, particularly in the congested 'key-way', inevitably leads to contact; similarly height can be a significant, even dominant, feature in the game today. However, FIBA's policy towards the rules of the game is to constantly seek to adapt and revise them so that players still exercise the powers of skill over brawn.

Basketball is a most complete sport, and an inherent quality is its attraction for big people and small people, aggressive players and technically skilful players, all of whom have a place in the game. It is harnessing together every one of these talents that creates the ultimate challenge, for essentially basketball is a team game.

We shall try throughout this book to demonstrate that in order to play basketball well you need to acquire skill, and that the quality and range of the skills you acquire is important to your success. You need to know the rules of the game so that you know what is permissible and you must set the quality of your team play above all else.

But what is it that sets this game apart from others? Well, for example, it is not subject to the vagaries of the weather; played indoors, there is very seldom any reason for cancellation. There are ten players to each team but, since only five may be on the court at any time, the organisation of the team presents less difficulties than with other team games. The fact that five players can play the game is in itself an advantage for, although it is always an advantage to have a full team, it is not mandatory. In addition, it is unlike most other team games for there is no such thing as a drawn game. At the end of a tied game teams must play extra periods until one wins.

But these are of course purely mechanical advantages. To discover what sets basketball apart from other games you have to play it – and we hope this book encourages you to do so and enriches your game.

SYMBOLS USED IN DIAGRAMS

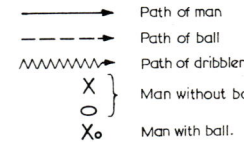

→ Path of man
-----→ Path of ball
ᗯᗯᗯᗯ→ Path of dribbler
X ⎫
O ⎬ Man without ball
X₀   Man with ball.

1 How to Start

Where basketball is played and joining a club

The odds are that most people have rarely if ever seen a game of basketball and know little about the rules. However, this is not a severe setback since anyone, when they know a little about how to play, can practise the skills by themselves – or with any number of additional players – for all one needs are the basic requirements: a ball and a ring. In US cities, all playgrounds are equipped with basketball courts, and New York playground basketball is famous throughout the basketball world. In the UK, however, very few individuals own basketballs or have backboards and rings fitted outside. In addition, few local authorities provide outdoor facilities. Therefore, in order to start, you will normally have to join your school team or a local youth team operating in a Further Education Centre, bona-fide Youth Centre, YMCA or YWCA, or those often organised by the larger basketball clubs. These school and youth teams normally all play friendly games with similar teams, but many also play in the school and youth leagues which operate throughout the country.

The kit required

Once you've decided that the game interests you, then there are certain items of necessary equipment. A first requirement is a reasonable pair of basketball boots/shoes or plimsolls: when you start to play you'll find that your feet take a considerable amount of punishment owing to the jumping, sprinting, turning and shuffling that are part of the techniques involved in the game, so you must buy good strong footwear. Boots and shoes specially made for basketball vary in price enormously.

In addition, you'll require shorts, a vest, socks and a sweater or, desirably, a tracksuit (many of our indoor facilities are inadequately heated). Once you start playing in a team, the vest and shorts have to be identical, of course, so the team administrator will probably provide the kit.

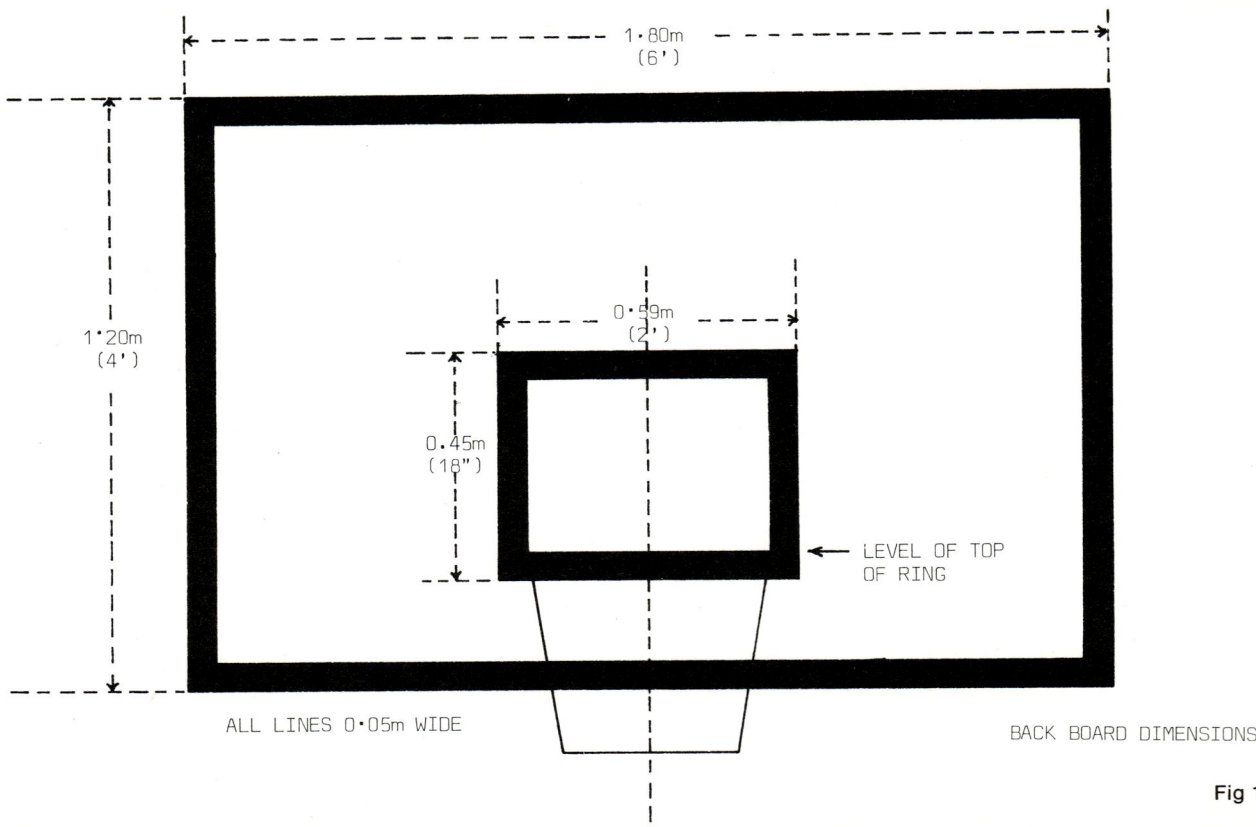

Starting your own team

Should you live in an area where basketball is not very popular or belong to a school or youth centre which does not have a team of its own, then you might consider forming your own club.

School teams are normally run at many age levels. Each school can affiliate to an area schools association which organises leagues, competitions and area representative teams. The area in turn affiliates to the relevant national schools association (see Appendix, page 101), and this association is responsible for the organisation of all aspects of schools basketball.

If there are no school leagues in the area, or you wish to start a youth or adult team, then basketball leagues playing in the evening and at weekends are often to be found, and it would be possible for a new team to join the appropriate junior or senior division of that league (players under 19 years of age on the 31st December of any year are classed as junior players and those over 19 years of age are classed as senior players). In addition, friendly games are often played with other local teams and also area and national competitions are arranged for all age levels.

Once it is decided to have a team then administra-

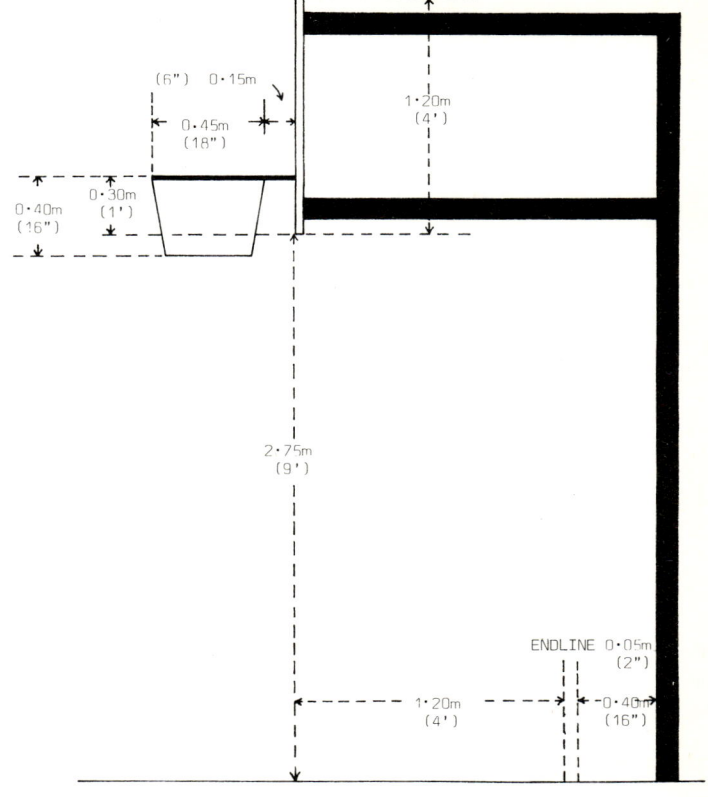

Fig 2   SIDE-ON VIEW OF THE BACKBOARD

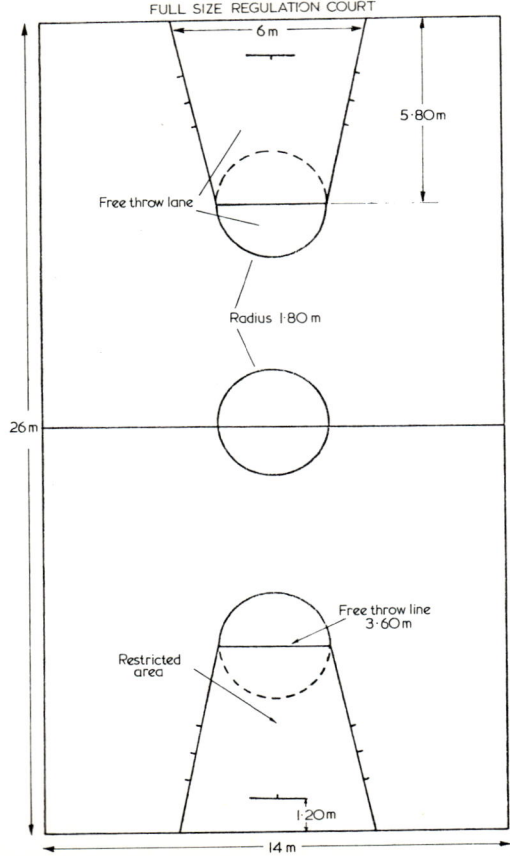

Fig 3

tors will be needed to run it. Someone has to write for fixtures, and to the local league secretary and the local basketball association in order to affiliate the club, register its players and pay the appropriate fees. This money has to be collected together with the club's national association affiliation fee and all the fees sent to the local secretary. There is often a fee to pay in order to join the local league, so that a club secretary/treasurer would be useful.

Further information and details of whom to write to are included at the end of the book in the Appendix, page 105.

Court layout and equipment

In order to start to play the game of basketball you need to understand the court layout; the accompanying pictures (Figures 1 to 3) show the detailed information you require. When you read the next chapter which explains the rules then you will be able to relate one with the other.

Other equipment you need to buy is:
- ☐ Several basketballs; normally one is kept for the 'match' ball and the others are used for practice balls.

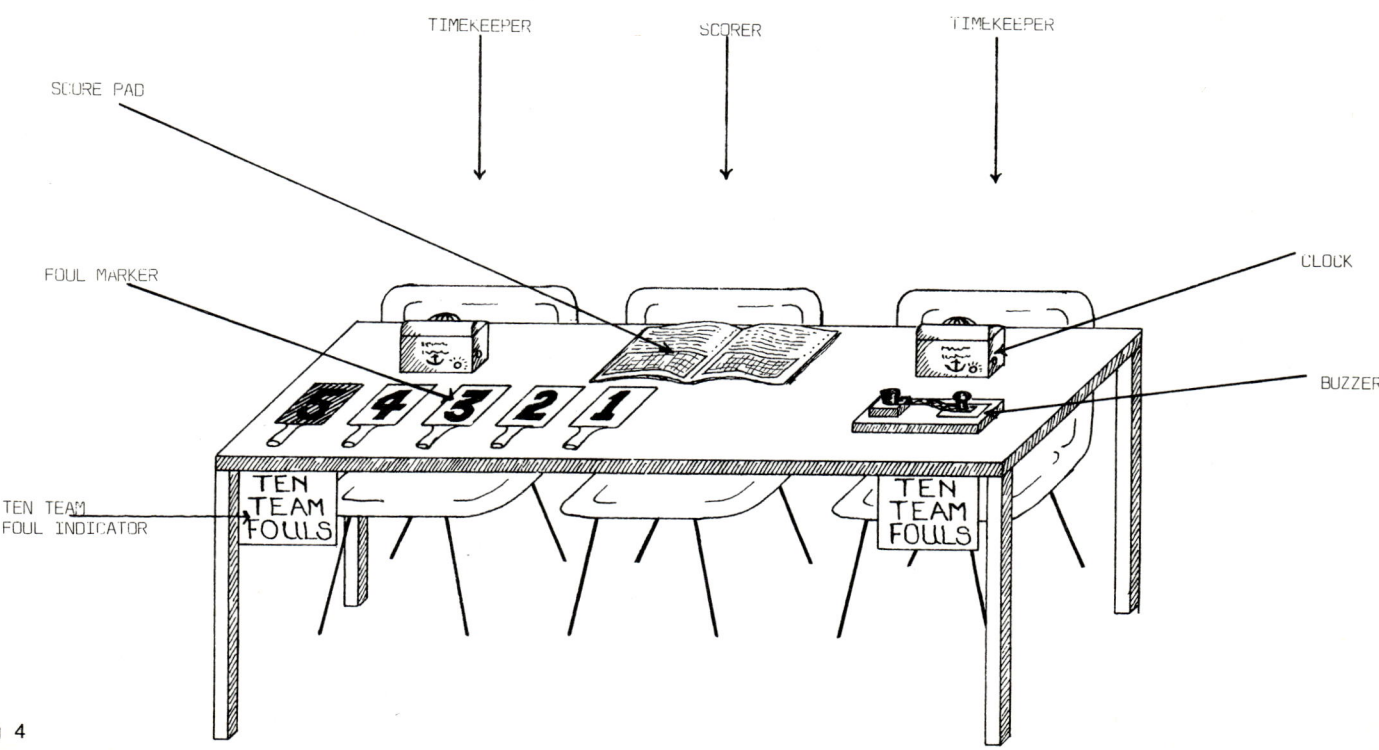

Fig 4

- ☐ Benches for the use of both teams before and during the game. The coach and substitutes will need to sit somewhere and have a central point for the team to gather for during-the-game coaching.
- ☐ Tables and chairs for the scorer, timekeeper and thirty-second operator.
- ☐ A game clock and thirty-second watch.
- ☐ The relevant association's official scoring pad.
- ☐ Bell or buzzer to mark the end of a time period.
- ☐ Foul-numbering system (numbers 1 to 5) to show the fouls committed by a player.
- ☐ Two large cards showing that 10 fouls have been made by one or both teams.

See Figure 4 which shows the timekeeper's table and highlights some of the equipment.

2 The Rules

As with most sports, basketball is played within a framework of 'dos' and 'don'ts'. Whether you are a player or a spectator, an understanding of this framework is vital if you are to enjoy and/or partake in a full way. Here follows an explanation of the important rules which currently govern the game for the Olympiad 1976-80. (Modifications to the rules may take place in each Olympic year and up-to-date rule books are published by the National Associations.)

Players, substitutes and coaches

Basketball is a team game consisting of 10 players (occasionally 12 in tournaments of certain kinds). During playing time there are five players from each team on the court and these may be substituted (i.e., one player replacing another) in certain situations which occur during a game. Players so substituted may themselves later return to the game in the same way.

As with many team sports, the players are numbered on both the front and the back. The numbers which may be used are from 4 to 15, with other numbers being permitted by some National Associations. In addition to the players, a team may also have a coach whose task is to help guide the team during the game. Normally he will sit at the side of the court with those members of the team who are not playing and will decide on substitutions, changes in team tactics and similar tasks.

Officials and their duties

Several officials help to control and administer a game of basketball. The two broad areas covered by these officials are:

	Area	Officials Responsible
1	to ensure that the game is played in accordance with the rules	referee and umpire
2	to record the score, fouls incurred by players, the time played etc., under guidance from the referee and umpire	scorer, timekeeper, and 30-second operator

Duties of the referee and umpire

The duties and powers of these officials fall into three time categories. The referee is the senior official and, throughout, any disputes between officials are settled by him.

Pre-game tasks

The referee approves the equipment to be used and ensures that the players' dress and footwear complies with the rules laid down.

During-the-game tasks

The referee and his co-official (the umpire) administer the rules throughout the game. Each official, using a whistle, has certain prescribed areas of responsibilities which change from end to end. (Figure 5.)

These responsibilities include interpreting the rules, deciding when a field goal or free throw has been made, signalling information on the scores made, the players scoring the baskets, fouls incurred and the player responsible for them and violations of the rules which take place. All of this he signals to the players, the officials and spectators. To do this he uses certain international signs.

After-the-game tasks

At the end of the game the referee checks the scorebook and signs it accordingly.

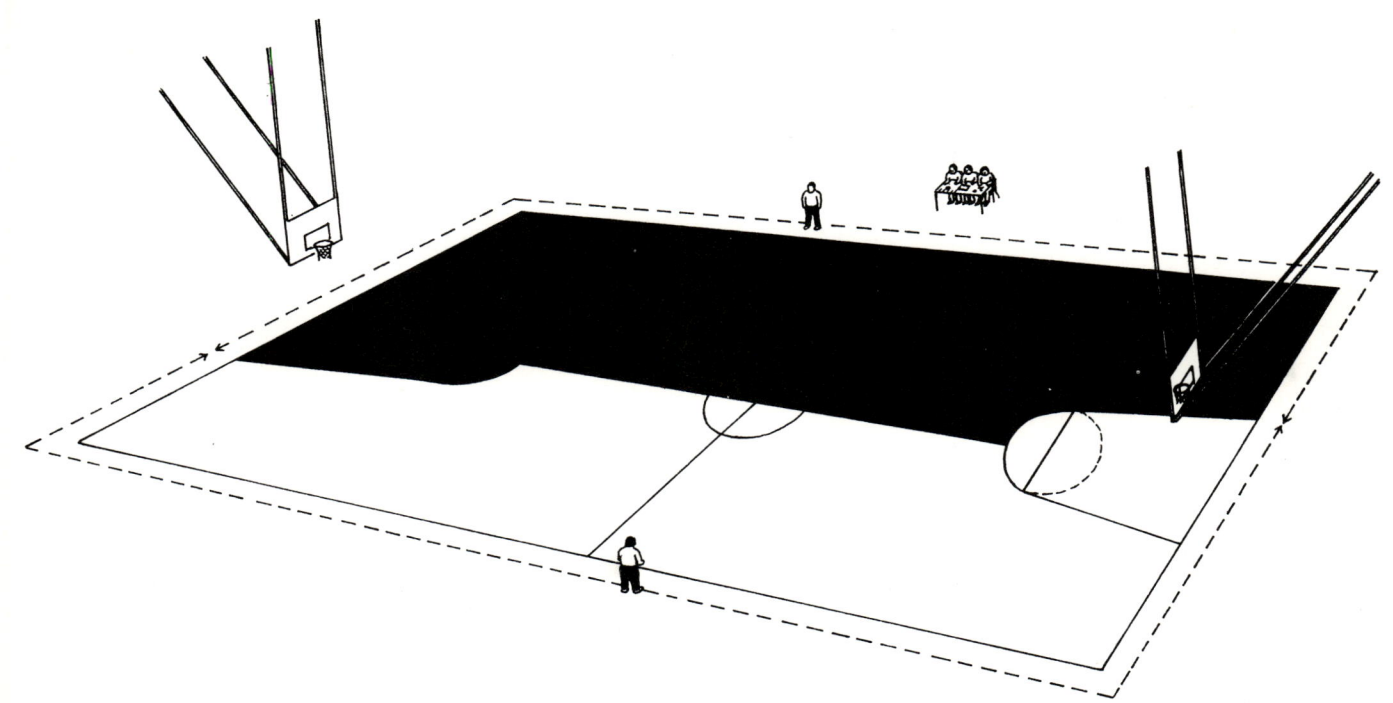

Fig 5

Fig 6

The Game

The game starts with five players from each team on the court and the referee throwing the ball between two of these at the centre circle. The team which gains possession from the jump-ball then has 30 seconds in which to try to score a basket (i.e., shoot the ball in such a way that it enters the ring from above and then passes through the ring, so scoring what is called a field goal, which is worth 2 points). To do this, any player may shoot from anywhere on court whenever he has the ball. However, it is considerably easier to score the closer a player is to the basket. Consequently, a team will attempt to bring the ball closer to the basket into which they are shooting before attempting to score.

This can be done in two ways. In the first instance, the player who has the ball may dribble the ball himself in any direction by bouncing the ball with either hand (but not both hands at the same time), or may pass the ball to a team-mate either before or after he has dribbled the ball.

Note that a player is only allowed to dribble the ball once (a dribble ends when a player touches the ball simultaneously with both hands or allows the ball to come to rest in either hand, at which point he can either pass or shoot) and is not allowed to run with the ball at any time during the game. A player may take a second dribble, however, if after having completed a dribble the ball goes out of his control, touches another player or the opponent's basket or backboard or is batted out of his control by an opponent.

The only foot movements the player with the ball is allowed to make are:

☐ Pivoting, the action of keeping one foot on the floor and in the same position whilst moving the other in any direction, any number of times (see Figure 6).

☐ At the end of a dribble, the player can choose to stop in two steps or, having taken two steps, must then either pass or shoot before he touches the floor again (see Figures 7 & 8).

Players without the ball can run or position themselves anywhere on the court so as to receive the ball from a team-mate except that they are not allowed to stay within the '3 second area' (see Figure 1 earlier) for longer than three consecutive seconds otherwise the official will blow his whistle, signal a violation of this rule and give possession of the ball to the other team. Similarly, a player may not leave the court (except as a natural part of the play) without the permission of an official.

The opposing team's task is to try to gain possession of the ball so that they may attempt to score at the opposite end of the court. To do this they may intercept a pass, take the ball away from a dribbling player, or catch or pick up the ball when an opponent fumbles it, when he has attempted to score and missed, when he allows the ball to go out of play for any reason or when he shoots and scores. In gaining possession, however, a player may not:

☐ Hold, push, charge, trip or impede the progress of his opponent by extending an arm, shoulder, hip or knee, by bending the body into other than a normal position or by using rough tactics (see Figure 9).

☐ Contact an opponent with his hand except where it is only the opponent's hand he touches. However, even this exception does not apply when an opponent is shooting.

☐ Guard from the rear such that contact results.

☐ Screen (i.e., attempt to prevent) a player from reaching a desired position or from reaching the ball if such an action causes contact between players.

Fig 7

Fig 8

☐ Strike the ball with his fist.
☐ Intentionally strike the ball with his leg or foot.

In the first four cases above, the opponent will be charged with a personal foul – which would be reclassed as an intentional foul if the contact made were considered to have been caused deliberately. Basketball is theoretically a 'no-contact' game but in certain situations (for instance, if two players go for a free ball and collide, with both players having made 'bonafide' attempts to play the ball) the contact made, no matter how serious, may be considered as accidental and need not be penalised.

In the other two cases, the player would have violated the rules and so possession of the ball would go to the other team.

Likewise, the team with the ball must act within the same restrictions or it will be similarly penalised. Also there is another 'don't':

☐ A dribbler shall not charge into or contact an opponent in his path nor attempt to dribble between two opponents or an opponent and a boundary line, unless there is sufficient room to do so without causing contact. However, if a dribbler establishes a path then an opponent cannot impede or obstruct that player unless he establishes a defensive posi-

Fig 9

tion (i.e., is standing in a normal way with two feet on the floor) with sufficient time for the dribbler to change direction and so avoid contacting him.

Throughout the game, therefore, first one team will attempt to progress the ball towards the basket in to which they are shooting and then attempt to score a basket, and then their opponents having gained possession, will attempt to do the same.

Playing regulations

Playing time and description of the game

The game shall consist of two halves of 20 minutes each with a 10 minute interval between halves. The team scoring the greatest number of points in the playing time shall win the game. If at the end of normal playing time, however, the score is a tie, then play shall be continued for an extra period of 5 minutes, or for as many such periods as is necessary to break the tie.

Five-second rule

If a player with the ball is so closely guarded that he is unable to pass, shoot or dribble within 5 seconds, then a held ball shall be called, with the two players involved having a jump ball at the centre or at one of the free throw lines, whichever is the nearest.

Ten-second rule

When a team gains control of the ball in its back court it must, within 10 seconds, cause the ball to go into its front court (i.e., to touch the floor or a player within the team's front court). If the team is unable to do this then a violation occurs and the ball is awarded to the other team, which throws the ball in from a point on the side line nearest to where the violation occurred.

Ball returning to the back court

If a player in his front court causes the ball to go into his back court (except in the situation of a jump-ball at the centre circle) and then he or a team-mate touches the ball in the back court before an opponent does so then a violation occurs and the opposing team is given a throw-in at the mid-point on the sideline.

Thirty-second rule

Earlier, the rule was mentioned whereby a team, having gained control of the ball on the court, must shoot within 30 seconds, failure to do so being a violation. However, if the ball goes out of court and the same team again has possession then a new 30-second period begins. Similarly if a team, having shot to score a basket, misses and then regains possession of the ball, a new 30-second period begins.

Rules of conduct

Technical foul

Both teams are required to play the game in a spirit of sportsmanship and fair play. If a player deliberately or repeatedly infringes this cooperation or spirit he is penalised by a technical foul. Situations which would lead to a technical foul being called include: disrespectfully addressing an official; using language or gestures likely to give offence; baiting an opponent by waving hands near his eyes; delaying tactics; or entering the court without permission from an official. When a technical foul is called against a player then this is recorded by the scorer against that player's name. The opposing team are awarded two free shots which can be taken by anyone in the offended team on the court at that time. These free shots are taken consecutively from the free throw line and each counts one point. Whether the first of these shots is successful or unsuccessful, if the second is successful then the opposing team get possession of the ball and bring it in from the end line. If the second of these attempts is unsuccessful then the ball comes into play with either team being allowed to get the rebounding ball and the normal rules applying after that. A technical foul may also be committed by the coach or one of the substitutes for similar offences to those described for a player technical foul. In this instance, however, the opponents are awarded only one free shot (worth again one point) and whether successful or not the offended team are then also given a throw-in from the mid-point of the side line.

Personal foul

Earlier, in the section headed 'The Game', personal fouls (i.e., player fouls which involve contact with an opponent) were described. The penalties for offences of this kind are similar to those for a technical foul by a player if the offence is committed on an opponent without the ball, an opponent who has the ball but is not in the act of shooting or an opponent who is shooting and does not score. However, if the player who is fouled was shooting and *did* score then, in addition to the two points awarded for the field goal, that player will also be awarded a free throw (again worth one point) with the ball coming into play as for the second free throw for a technical foul described earlier. If the player is fouled in the act of shooting and misses, he is then given three shots from which he has the chance of making two.

If an opponent deliberately fouls a player then the same rules will apply as in the case of a personal foul but the scorer will record that the personal foul was intentional. In all of these situations, however, it is the player who was fouled who must take the free shots at basket himself.

Double foul

A double foul is a situation in which two opponents commit fouls against each other at approximately the same time. A personal foul will be charged against each offending player and the game re-started by a jump ball between the two offending players unless a valid field goal was scored and then the ball is awarded to the opposing team to bring in from the end line.

Multiple foul

This is the situation in which two or more teammates commit personal fouls against the same opponent at approximately the same time. Personal fouls will be charged against each of the offending players and two free shots given to the player who was fouled and administered as with a single personal foul. If the player was in the act of shooting then again each opponent will be charged a personal foul with the situation administered as with a personal foul.

Disqualifying foul

A player may be disqualified from the game for any flagrant unsportsmanlike act or for repeatedly committing a technical foul. His team may immediately bring on a substitute for him.

Five fouls by a player

A player who has committed five fouls (either personal or technical) must automatically leave the game. As in the case of a disqualifying foul, however, the team is allowed to immediately bring on a substitute for that player.

Ten fouls by a team

After a team has scored 10 player fouls (either technical or personal) in any half of the game then all subsequent player fouls shall be penalised by two free throws which will be administered in the usual way.

Well, those are the 'dos' and 'don'ts' of basketball. As in the case of many games, it looks like a daunting list, but you will find that the more you watch and play the game then the more the pieces of the jigsaw fit together. As was stated earlier, basketball is essentially a non-contact game and the rules and their interpretation by the officials will be towards penalising physical contact, so that the ball-playing and team skills described in the succeeding chapters predominate during a game.

3 Individual Skills

Basketball is a game in which both individual and team skills are equally important. Teamwork provides the opportunity for a player to score, but it is that player himself who must have the skill to receive the ball, take on his defender(s) and shoot the ball into the basket. If he fails to score then the team will have nothing to show for its ability to create the scoring situation. In this chapter we will concentrate on individual skills and explain what a player needs to be able to do well in order to partake in the game fully both as an individual and, equally importantly, as a member of the team.

In essence, the aim in basketball is for a *team* to get possession of the ball and then, again as a *team*, to take the ball to the other basket and score. In order to win, a team has to accomplish this more times than its opponents, and to do this requires better ball control in

☐   passing and receiving the ball,
☐   dribbling the ball, and
☐   shooting and scoring

when you are attacking; as well as better

☐   defending

when your opponents have the ball.

Throughout the remainder of this chapter we will explain, one at a time, the important facets of each of these *individual* skills.

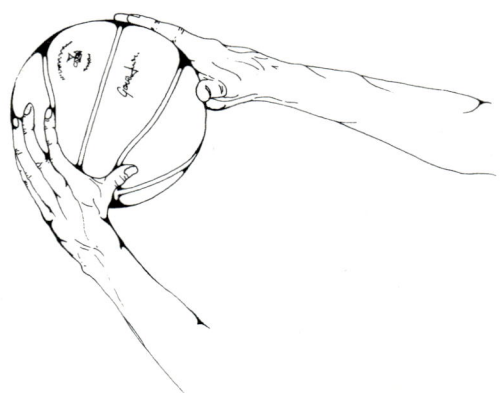

Fig 10

Passing

Passing and receiving the ball are two skills which must be given great attention by players. The glamour is in shooting but, if you are unable to get the ball to the shooter or as a shooter you are unable to receive the variety of passes thrown at you, then, of course, your shooting ability is of little help – you cannot shoot without the ball!

Basketball is a game of finger-tip control. Figure 10 shows the ball and your grip on it – you should spend time getting to know the ball itself by spinning it, flipping it up in the air, and generally being able to handle it as though it were on a piece of string – the greater your control the better you will be as a player.

The most commonly used passes are illustrated now in Figures 11 to 15. It is most important, with all passing, to incorporate the following points in all that you do:

☐ pass early, fast and accurately,
☐ use fakes (eyes, slight movements of the head, shoulders, foot or hip) in order to make it easier
☐ don't telegraph your pass,
  to pass to your team-mate,

Fig 11

29

Fig 12

- don't fix your eyes on the receiver of your pass – the defenders will know where it is going,
- but, equally, don't look one way and pass another your team-mate may have moved,
- pass and move – it is easier for the defender if you just stand still,
- don't force passes – you have to know that the pass is going to get to its destination,
- be alert – keep your head moving so that you know where you want to pass the ball before you receive it from a team-mate, and
- know your passing lanes.

Techniques to remember when passing

Fingers and wrist – follow through the pass – extend your arms – palms down – don't bend your elbows too much.

Why pass?

To pull opponents out of defensive position, to release your own players for a drive to the basket or a shot, to create a better angle for a pass in to another team-mate nearer the basket, and to keep your defenders moving.

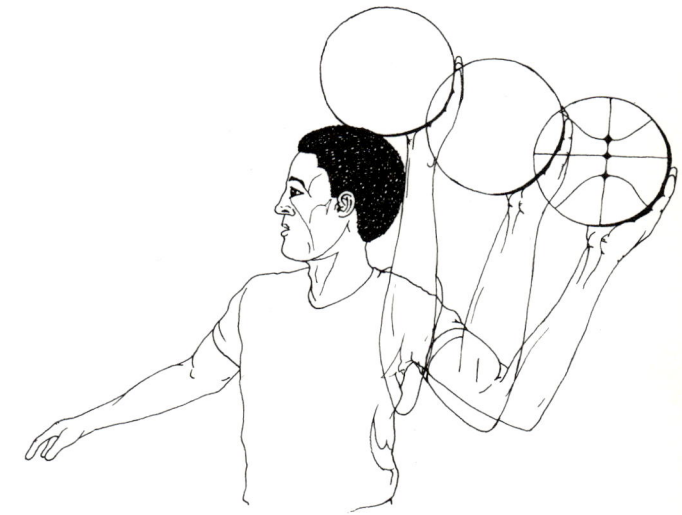

Fig 13

Fig 14

Receiving

You need good hands and anticipation, quick feet and an alert mind to be able to free yourself when it is necessary to receive the ball. While we have emphasised good accurate passing, it is inevitable that under match conditions you will have a great variety of passes thrown at you, high, low, wide, fast, slow, awkward, all testing your ability to receive them and then, with the minimum delay, make your pass to a team-mate or your shot for the basket.

In order to help the passer you can
- meet the ball – move to the ball and extend your arms,
- protect the passing lane – try to keep a lane open between the passer and yourself,
- show a target – see Figure 16,
- watch the ball into your hands – don't look for your shot until you have that ball, safe and sound, and
- relax – it is easier to catch the ball if your hands are not rigid.

Fig 15

Shooting

Scoring baskets is the end result of all the individual and team skills and is probably the most important single skill in the game. You will develop your own preferences, but it is essential to master the techniques of shooting in order that your shooting is effective under pressure and at whatever level you play. It is most important that all your team are able to score – if you cannot shoot you will be the weak link in your team chain and the opposition can afford to let you alone when your side is attacking.

Correct technique in shooting is vital; it not only develops accuracy but also means that you can shoot from further out and this makes it more difficult for your defender to mark you. A thoroughly practised technique can be effective under pressure, and so it is essential to practise your shooting; we recommend that initially you perfect lay-ups, normally a very high percentage shot because it is very close to the basket, before venturing on to jump shots, hook shots, etc., which are more difficult to perform with an acceptable level of accuracy in an actual game. The lay-up is also important because it incorporates movement with the ball, jumping, balance, control and accuracy, all of

Fig 16

which are critical individual skills which you have to use throughout a game.

The lay-up shot

Figure 18 shows the action to complete the lay-up shot – notice that when you have completed a dribble or have received the ball on the run, you are allowed *two* steps before having to release the ball (refer to Chapter 2, page 19).

If you are right-handed you receive the ball or stop your dribble as your left foot comes to the ground (you will find that on some occasions you have to adjust your feet just before catching the ball).

You now take a stride on your right foot and jump up towards the basket from your left foot on your second step, at the same time taking the ball up in two hands and releasing it at the top of your jump from an extended arm.

Try to ensure
- ☐ a quite definite and loud two count,
- ☐ that you watch the basket all the time,
- ☐ that you aim to put the ball on the top corner of the black rectangle on the backboard,
- ☐ that you release the ball at maximum height,
- ☐ that you release the ball from a straight arm,

Fig 17

Fig 18

- that you release finally from your first and second fingers,
- that you follow through with soft relaxed fingers, and that
- your body follows through under the basket.

Set-shot, free-shot (foul-shot), jump-shot

The principles governing these shots are the same as for the lay-up and, if you can accept, absorb and put into practice these concepts then you will find that your shooting skills will improve more easily. Young players, particularly playing with a full-size ball, will lack the strength and technique to perform good jump-shots (especially from 5 metres or more), but the principles governing the set-shot will allow you to develop your jump-shot eventually.

A good way to develop your shooting skills is to choose two or three spots on the court from which you will usually tend to shoot and then to practise from those spots – if you find you cannot score from that spot then go closer, until you can easily reach the basket. Remember that if you are too far away from the basket you will find it more difficult to practise your techniques. If you don't shoot from a spot in practice then you shouldn't shoot from there in a match.

The following points establish a charter which you should follow every time to be successful at these types of shot:

- CONCENTRATE,
- square stance,
- flexed knees,
- ball held in front of and above the head,
- non-shooting hand acts as a stabiliser,
- the 'V' shape between your thumb and forefinger is lined up with the basket,
- wrist-elbow lined up with basket, wrist cocked, elbow leading,
- soft fingers with the ball resting on pads and your fingers spread out,
- the ball is released finally from the first and second fingers – feel the slight backspin,
- the shot is taken with a long, straight and high arm,
- the wrist bends and flags after the shot has been made,
- watch either the front rim OR rear rim OR the hole in the middle of the basket,
- go for height – get a good arc with the shot,

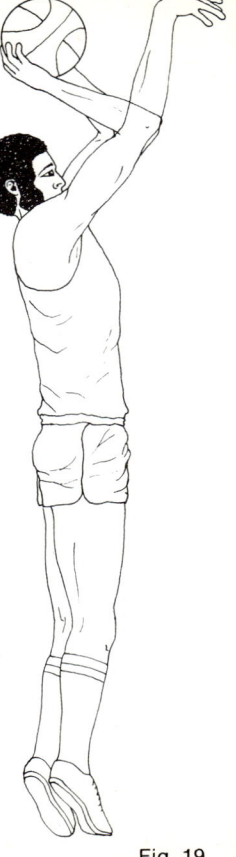

Fig 19

Fig 20

☐ the follow-through will involve a slight but controlled forward lean.
☐ Follow the same procedure each time: this will give you
☐ CONFIDENCE

You must never forget – if you don't shoot you won't score.

Dribbling

It is as important to have good ball-handlers (dribblers) in your team as it is for a soccer team to have players able to hold the ball. Apart from the glamour and spectator-appeal of a dribbler, it is of immense value for the team to have players with the ability to go on their own, to hold the ball under pressure and to do the unexpected when the defence has gained an advantage over the attackers. You must, however, be able to recognise the difference between the player who dribbles for the sake of dribbling (often called a ball-hog) and the player whose dribbling is used for the benefit of the team.

There are two types of dribbling, the low dribble as in Figure 21 which is used when you are under pressure and the high dribble which is used usually when

Fig 21

you are clear and running to the basket – Figure 22.

Within the two groups there are several ways of dribbling the ball some of which are illustrated here.

Why do you dribble?
- ☐ To move forward into attack,
- ☐ to create space for a team-mate,
- ☐ to play out time at the end of the game when your team is winning ('a stall'),
- ☐ to attack your defensive player,
- ☐ to draw fouls by tempting the defensive player to take the ball from you,
- ☐ to create space for yourself in order to shoot or to pass, or
- ☐ to get out of a tight situation.

Dribbling is a skill which must be practised – the more you practise the better you will be as a ball handler. In order to develop your skill remember, and work on, the following points:
- ☐ finger-tip control – squeeze the ball down and follow it with your hand,
- ☐ you should work on *both* hands – if you can only dribble with one hand then you can normally

Fig 22

42

only move in one direction, which makes it easier for your defender,
- protect the dribble by placing your body between the defensive player and the ball and also by keeping the free elbow held up,
- don't watch the ball; keep your head up – if you can't see your team mates you can't pass to them,
- dribble low in tight situations,
- dribble high for speed when free, with the ball in front and outside the line of the body,
- vary the speed of your dribbling, and
- practise feinting – faking before and during your dribble.

Individual defence

This is a critical and sadly neglected part of the game. There is a place in many teams for an outstanding defender – although, of course, the glamour is attached to shooting and scoring! You should take pride in defending well and gain great satisfaction from knowing that you are performing defensive skills well. Remember that to win you have to score more points than your opponents, and good defence contributes significantly to this aim – and makes it more difficult for your opponents.

Fig 23

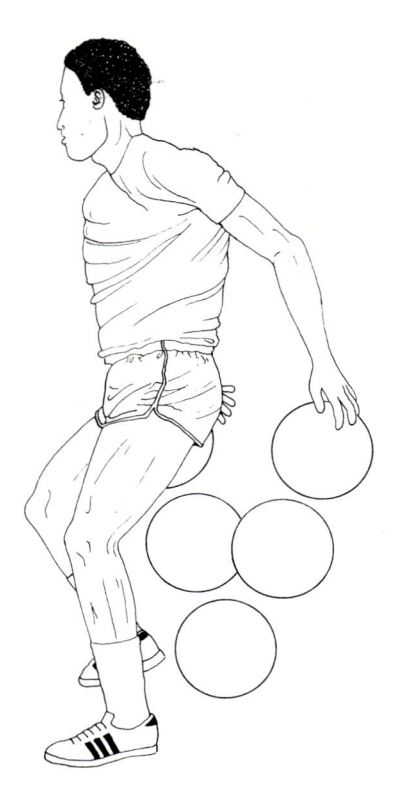

Fig 24

Fig 25

You have to ask three questions when defending:
- [ ] where is my player?,
- [ ] where is the ball?, and
- [ ] where is the basket I am defending?

When you consider your responsibilities as a team defender you have to add to your *individual* responsibilities that of being a helper *to the rest of your team*.

Once you are aware of your responsibilities you know that you have to defend against:
- [ ] the man with the ball,
- [ ] the post player,
- [ ] the player nearest the ball (1st receiver) – see Figure 26, and
- [ ] players who are more than one pass from the ball (2nd receivers) – see Figure 27.

You defend against each of these in a different way, as illustrated.

Stance – against the ball-holder
- [ ] Feet to be shoulder-width apart,
- [ ] weight taken along the inside of the foot, ball-heel, to make movement easier,
- [ ] knees bent – sitting position,
- [ ] arms bent – palms up,
- [ ] head up – watch his number,

Fig 26

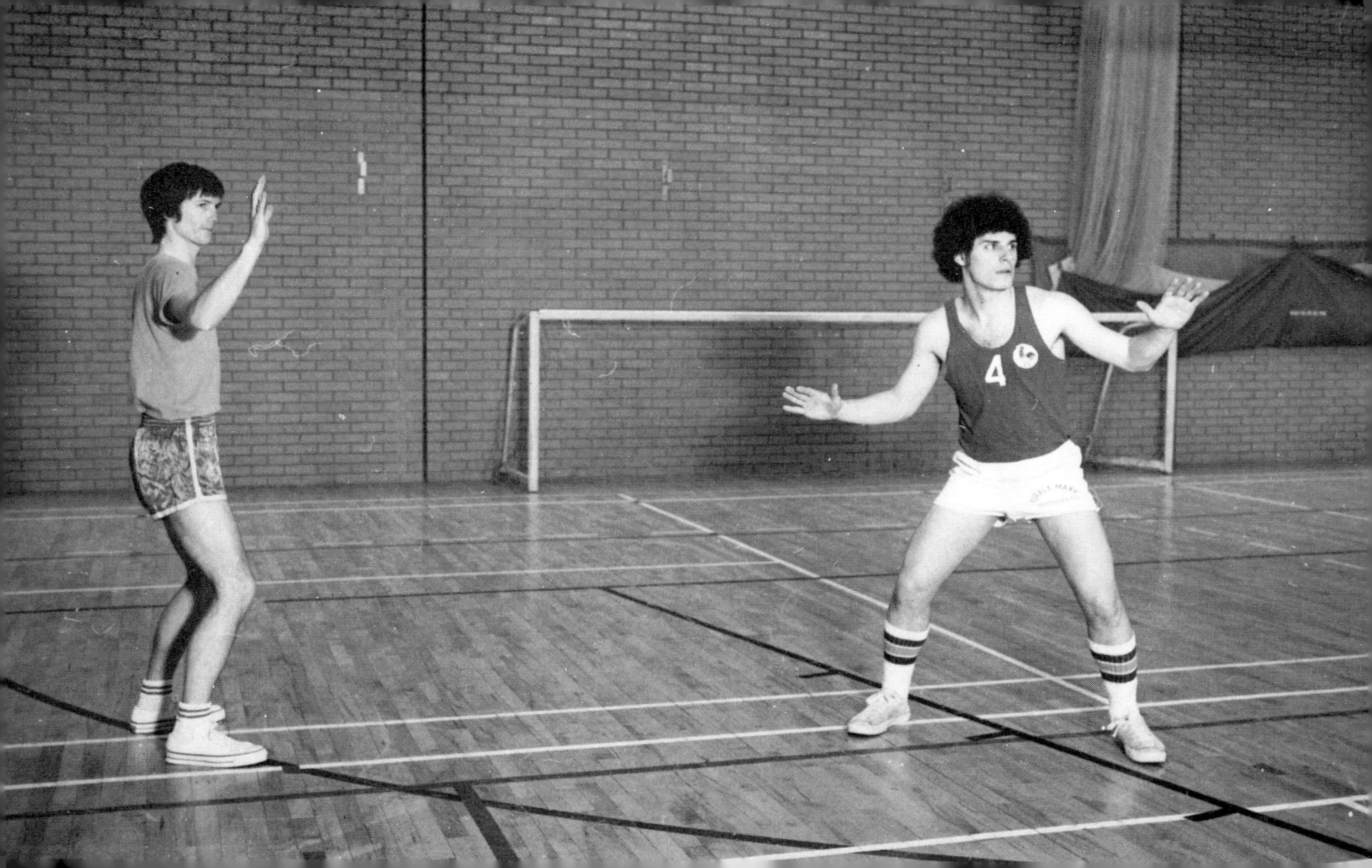
4

- [ ] but your eyes are active and you see ALL,
- [ ] crabwise shuffle – feet never less than shoulder-width apart,
- [ ] if he is within shooting range (Figure 28) you must protect the drive and prevent the shot,
- [ ] maintain a 60–90cm distance, and
- [ ] try to keep him within your knees.

Stance – against first receiver
- [ ] Feet shoulder-width apart,
- [ ] knees bent – sitting position,
- [ ] one arm up denying pass – other arm 'feeling' for player – don't let him get out of contact,
- [ ] get into and pressure his passing lane (i.e., the route the ball will take if a pass is made to him),
- [ ] crabwise shuffle – feet should never be less than shoulder-width apart, maintain a distance of 60 to 90 centimetres from your opponent, and
- [ ] watch the ball and be aware of the player.

Stance – against second receiver
- [ ] More relaxed,
- [ ] place yourself in such a position that if the ball is passed to your man you could intercept it, and
- [ ] have hands and arms ready to intercept.

Fig 28

Fig 29 and 30

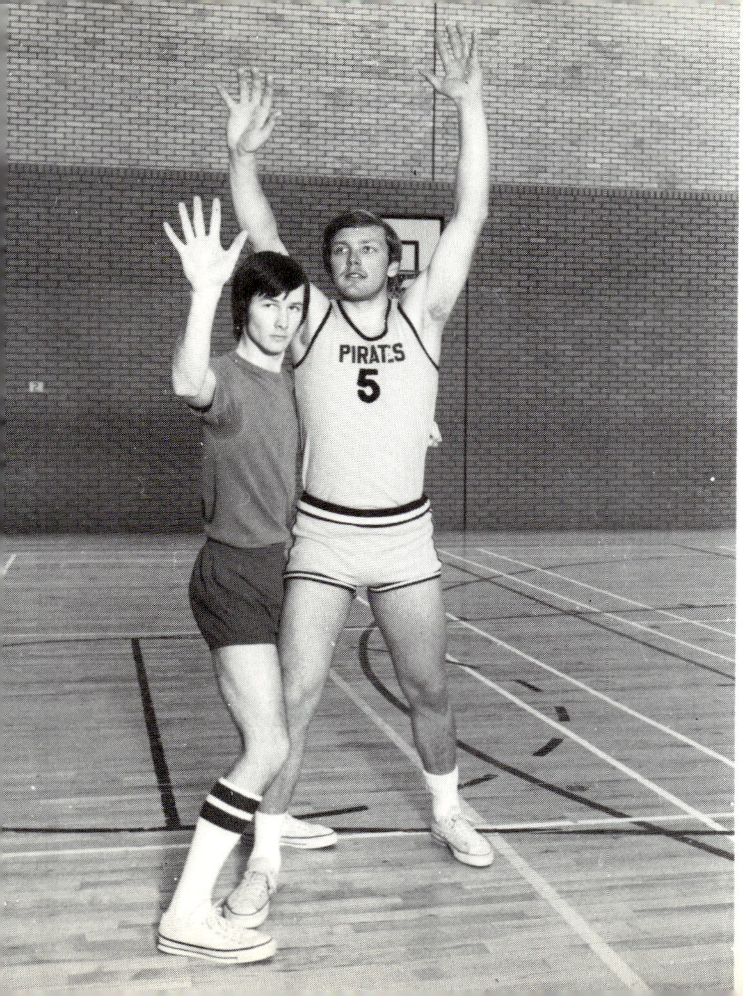
5

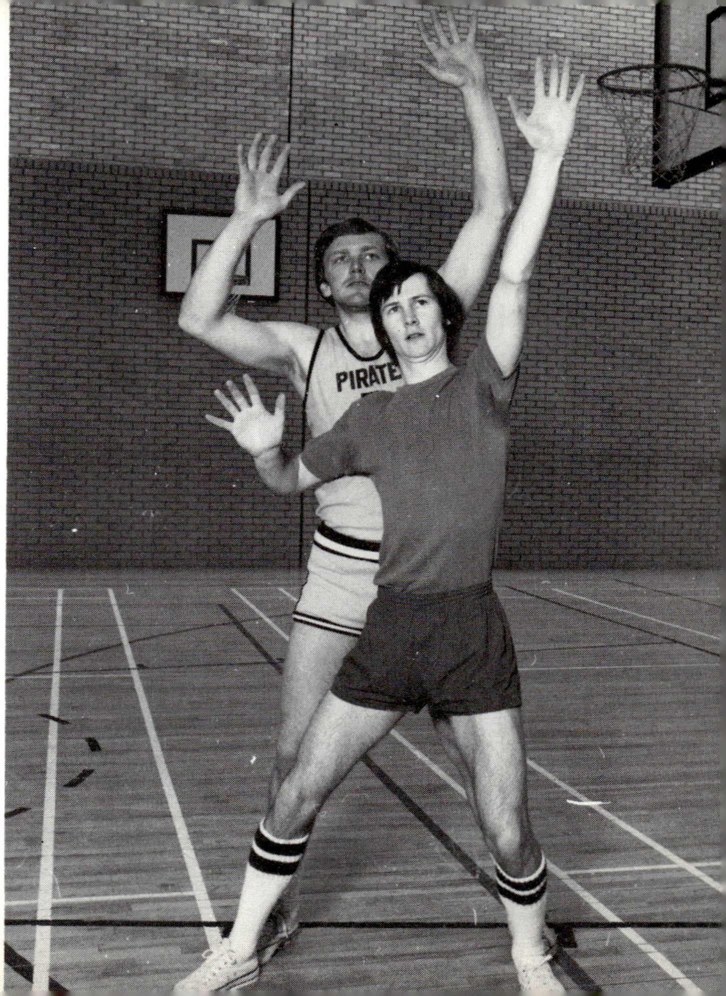

Stance – *against the post player*

The post player should be defended against differently according to the position he takes up.

If he assumes a position at high post the defender guards him from the high side to prevent the ball getting to him from a high forward position (See Figure 29).

If he takes a middle post the defender pivots on the right foot and brings the left foot and arm through to 'front' the post (See Figure 30).

At low post the defender comes on to the baseline side of the post by pivoting on his left foot and driving his right arm and leg through. He should now be able to prevent the post player driving along the baseline (See Figure 31).

If he takes up a position at centre you defend behind him but adjust your position according to the position of the ball while keeping an arm in front of the post player to deny the pass in (See Figure 32).

As with most games, there is much to learn in order to become an accomplished player. However, whether practising or playing carry the points discussed in this chapter in mind until you do them automatically. Some skills, no doubt, will come more easily to you

Fig 31

and some will be more difficult to acquire. Remember, though, that it is important to develop an all-round set of skills and so you must practise not only the things you are good at but also the things which you find difficult to do, while being prepared to practise and develop a skill over a long period of time so that you can do it naturally during a game.

Fig 32

4 Team Defence

The techniques of individual defence have been described in the last chapter, and it is on this individual skill that effective team defence is based. Earlier, too, it was explained that the glamour in basketball is in scoring baskets and that defence tends to lack glamour. However, you can derive considerable personal and team satisfaction from defending well.

Defending well means hard physical and mental work – you have to know where the ball is and where your opponents are, your feet arms and eyes should be always moving, and the good defender maintains an incessant chatter to his team-mates – 'helping by talking'.

It may well be that determination and courage are the most important skills in defence. 'We want the ball,' is a sound motto for any team. Once the ball is on the backboard you must rebound hard, catch cleanly and immediately start an attack. You will normally find that it is easier to run when you are attacking than when you have to defend. In this chapter we describe different methods of defence and it is to your advantage to try each type before deciding which best suits your team.

Patterns of defence

There are three types of defence:

- *Zone defence*, the aim of which, as its name implies, is to defend the three-second area, and thus the basket.
- *Man-to-man defence* which again, as the name implies, requires each individual defender to be responsible for an attacker but usually also operates around the defensive three-second area.
- *Pressure Defences*: a 'press' defence can take the form of man-to-man or zone, and will generally be initiated away from your three-second area, sometimes in your opponents' half and sometimes just inside your own half.

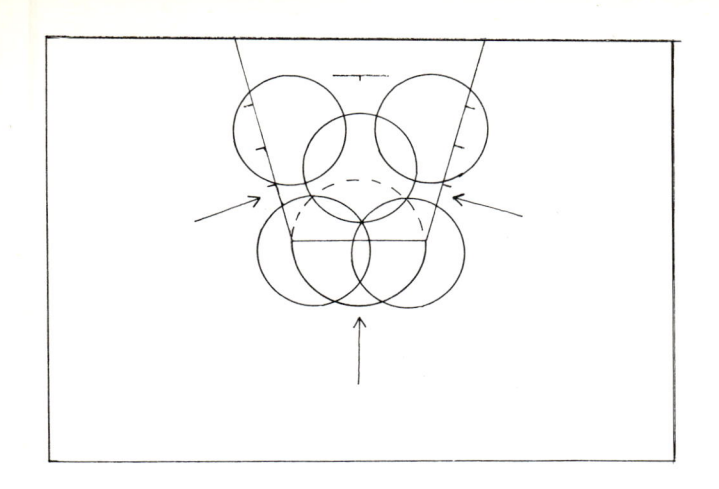

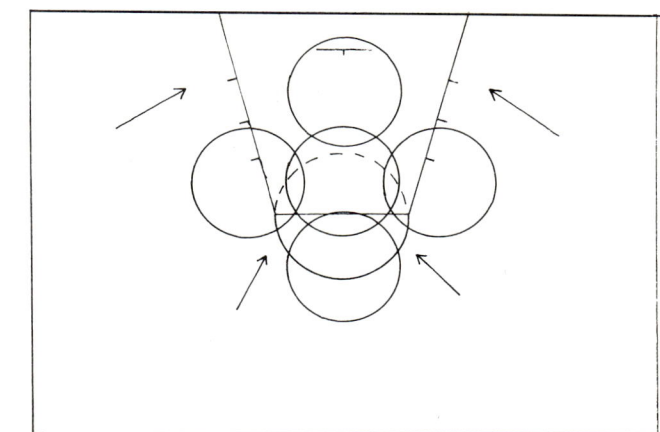

Fig 33 (See symbols on p 8)

Fig 34

There are, naturally, combinations of defence where you start with a press and fall back into a zone or a man-to-man defence.

Zone defence

In this type of defence each player has a predetermined position to occupy and area to defend. Generally your biggest players will be central or baseline defenders and your smaller, quicker players will occupy positions at the head of the 'key'. There are several types of zone defences, and four of the more common types are illustrated here. Whichever zone defence you play, you must be aware that each depends upon speed, mobility, pressure and anticipation.

All zone defences aim to prevent the opponents from receiving, dribbling or shooting the ball close to your basket. Consequently, they force attacking players to shoot from outside the key way or three-second

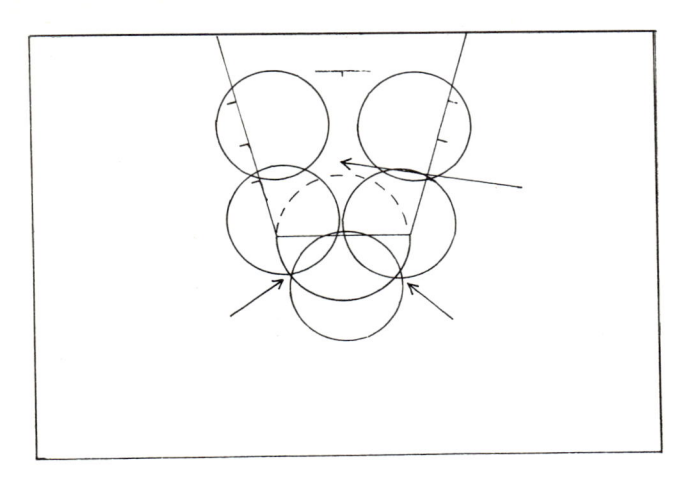

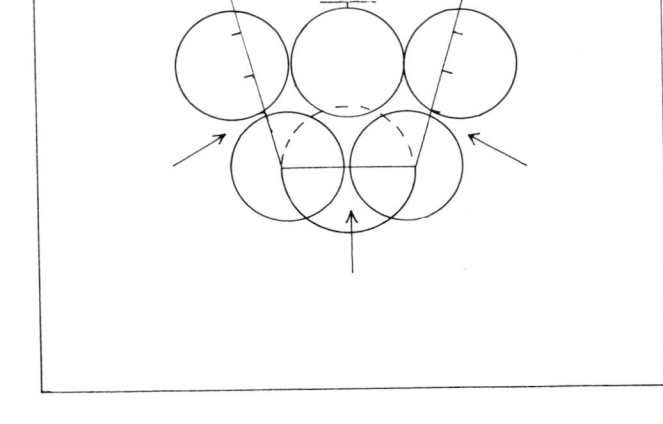

Fig 35

Fig 36

area; this is the aim of the defending team on the principle that shots taken from longer distances achieve a lower percentage scoring rate. Once the ball is passed to a man near the basket (especially if he is a big man) then it is difficult to prevent him legally from scoring. Your zone defence is designed to prevent this happening and that is why you must put pressure on the ball-holder and make passing difficult for him, especially to a man near the basket. That is why your team-mates must place themselves in the best possible position to stop the pass.

There are many combinations of zone defence (interpret the numbers from the head of the key towards the baseline). Four are shown and their weaknesses illustrated.

1. 2–1–2 (Figure 33)
2. 1–3–1 (Figure 34)

3. 1–2–2   (Figure 35)
4. 2–3   (Figure 36)

You will use each one in different circumstances but be aware that each one requires speed, mobility, aggression, pressure and anticipation. In English basketball the reasons for playing a zone are not necessarily the reasons that a coach would wish to give us. Some English teams just cannot play against a zone – so that becomes a good enough reason.

Some general rules when playing a zone defence are:
☐ Anticipate – deny the *pass* and the *shot;*
☐ pressurise the ball holder but don't go for the ball – you have to judge between a possible steal against a probable foul on the attacker;
☐ defend your area – close the gaps; and
☐ remember you are a helper to the rest of your team.

Some individual techniques for players are:
☐ Watch both the ball and the opposing players;
☐ develop all-round vision;
☐ move your feet quickly in a crabwise shuffle and always keep them at least a shoulderwidth apart;
☐ arms up in defence – keep them bent with your palms up;
☐ crouch low – you have to defend against the pass and the dribble; and
☐ anticipate – watch the ball-handler's eyes and arms for any clue as to what he may do.

Man-to-man defence

Here, each defender is primarily responsible for marking one attacker. His tasks are to know always where his man is and to keep between his man and the basket.

Problems arise when, as you move while defending against an attacker (with or without the ball), he runs you into a screen (see Figure 37) in order to lose you and so be able to receive a pass, to drive or to shoot without you pressing him. There are many ways an attacker can do this and some are described in Chapter 5. Your options as a defender in this situation are:
☐ To try to go over the screen but not too far from your attacker;
☐ If you can't, your team-mate must leave room for you to go immediately behind the screen (Figure 38); or

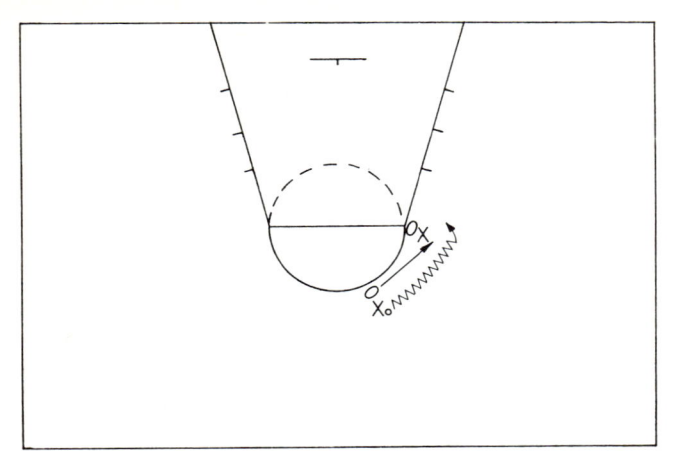

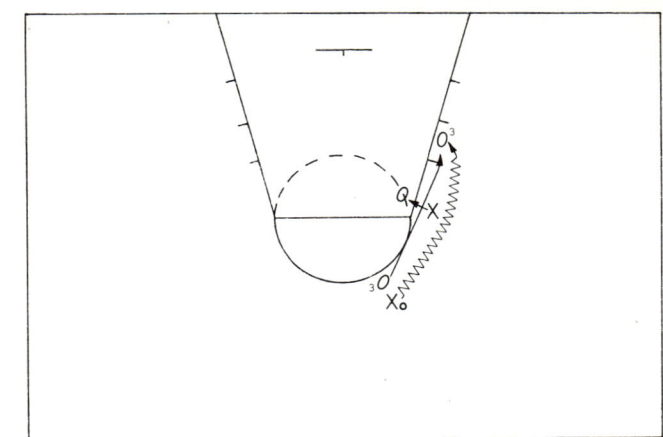

Fig 37

Fig 38

☐ If you have actually run into the screen your team-mate, seeing this, will then (and only then) switch to your man while you switch to his man (Figure 39). (Note: always avoid the apparently *easy* switch for fear of creating a mis-match [see Chapter 7].)

There are also situations where your attacker will cut to the basket, fake to go one way before going the other, move out to take a pass, and so on. At all times you must be alert and, as described in the section on individual defence (see page 43), take up the appropriate position.

In order to give you a picture of what tends to happen, Figure 40 shows a typical attacking formation with X team here playing a 1–3–1 offence. Team O are defending man-to-man and you can see that O with their arms out are making it very difficult for X to get the ball to his team-mates close to the basket.

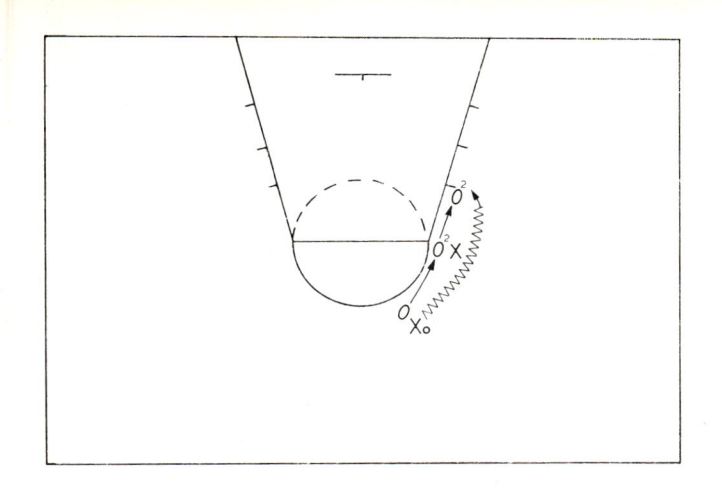

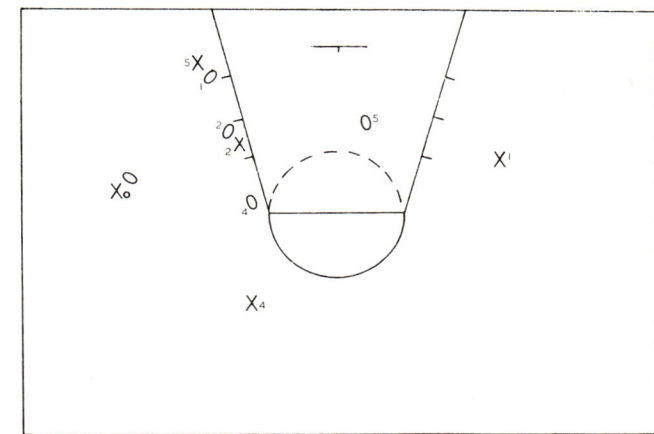

Fig 39

Fig 40

O4 has sagged off X4 in order to help O3 and O2 if necessary. He has his arm across in the passing lane from XO to X2's left hand. If XO passes the ball back out to X4 the immediate danger is over and O4 has time to get to X4's spot at the same time as the ball.

Meanwhile O5 has placed himself strategically in the keyway to help O1 and O2, should XO throw a high pass, and also in position to prevent a long pass reaching X1. Should the ball be passed out to X4 and round to X1 the picture would change.

As the ball moves round, so the post player probably moves across the keyway and the new 1–3–1 pattern is established.

Pressure defence

For obvious reasons the name for this defence is shortened to 'press'. It takes the form either of a zone or of man-to-man defence.

57

You use a press when you want to disrupt the opposition and get possession of the ball as quickly as possible. Usually, the team gaining possession of the ball can bring the ball up in a leisurely unpressured way, and the press gives you the opportunity to throw a 'spanner in the works'. Possession of the ball is gained by the defending team in many ways including:
- ☐ the ball is stolen from the ball-handler;
- ☐ the ball-handler is forced into making a violation (e.g., a double dribble or carrying the ball);
- ☐ the ball-handler makes a loose pass and this is intercepted by his opponents or it goes out of bounds.

The key here is for the defenders not to commit a foul going for a 'steal' on the ball-handler or in trying to intercept a pass to another player, but to apply continuous pressure and to be patient.

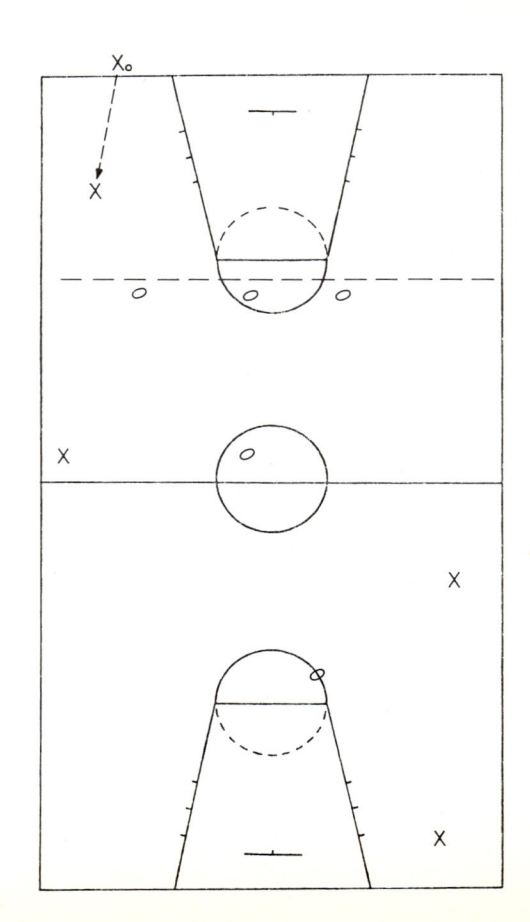

Fig 41

Fig 42

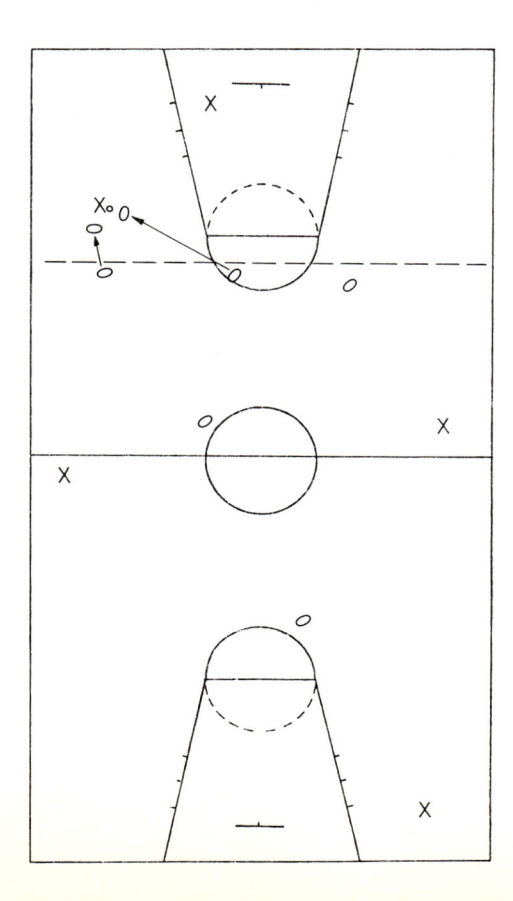

Zone press

There are many types of zone press. We have taken as an example the 1–1–3 press.

You will see from Figure 41 that the players are spread initially to cover the depth of the court. In theory, the opposition is allowed to make the first pass unopposed provided, of course, that it occurs inside the shaded area. It is hoped that O1 starts to dribble, at which stage the two nearest X players close in on him. X1 denies him room down to the side line and X2 traps him from the side. X1 and X2 try to prevent O1 dribbling or passing and hope to gain possession of any loose ball which may arise as a result of this pressure (Figure 42). They have to be

59

careful to avoid contact and, therefore, the temptation of reaching in and across their opponent for the ball must be avoided – only go if the ball is free.

Meanwhile the other defenders all move to create better positions for themselves in relation to the attackers. The defenders' aim is to intercept any ball thrown hastily or inaccurately from the ball-holder to one of his team-mates.

If the ball-holder does not bounce the ball, the defenders wait for the pass but use their bodies and arms to create as impassable a barrier as they can. The remaining defenders adjust their positions to take account of other attackers so that they can intercept the loose pass, or put pressure on the player who next receives the ball.

Once again the players nearest the ball apply pres-

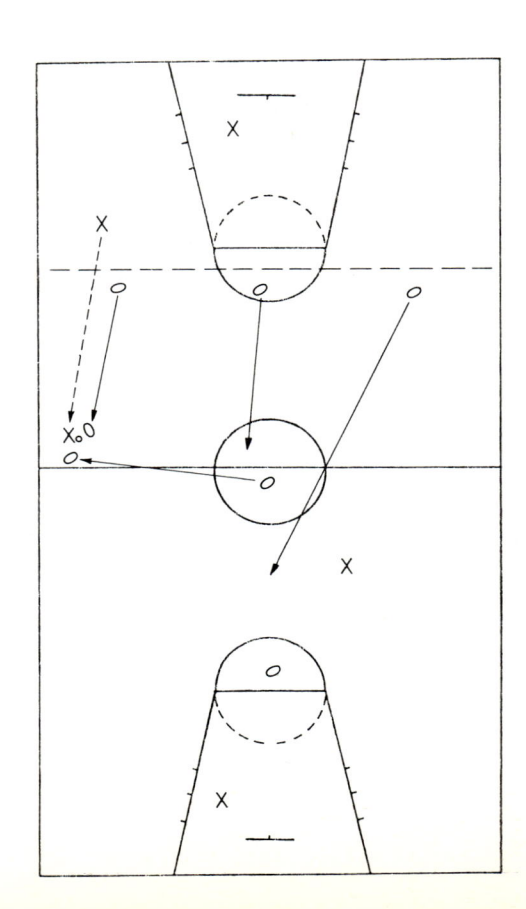

Fig 43

Fig 44

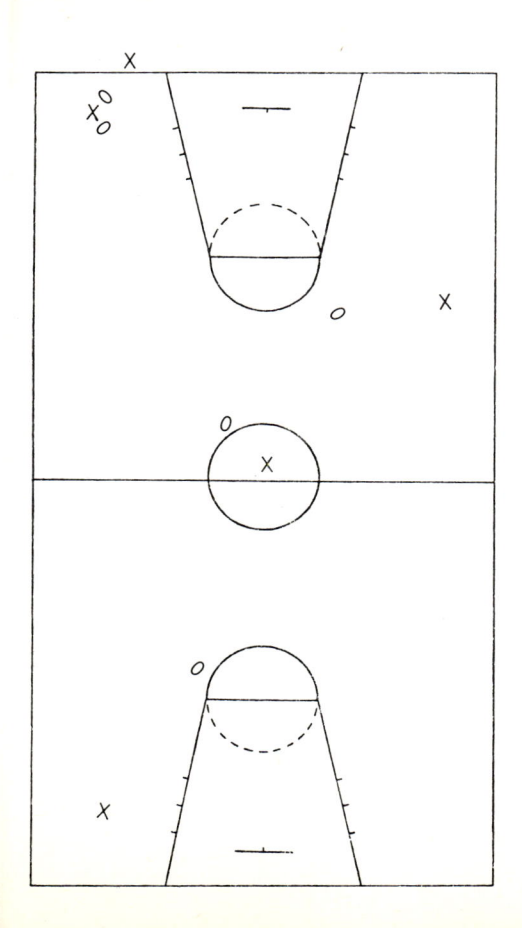

sure and the remaining players take up fresh positions (Figure 43).

Man-to-man press

In this type of press each defender marks an attacker. You will either predetermine who you mark or you will pick up the nearest man to you, whichever method your team decides upon.

All the normal rules for individual and team man-to-man defence apply in this case.

You will see from Figure 44 that it is not necessary to mark the man who is to bring the ball into play. Sometimes teams put two men to cover the man who is nearest this player and therefore the most likely to receive the first pass. Often the player bringing the ball into play has to make a long pass or has difficulty

61

in passing at all to a team-mate – if you remember, the rule is that he is allowed only five seconds to make that first pass. The other defensive players will take up positions so that they can see the player they are marking as well as the ball, and if possible stand in a position where they could intercept a pass.

We have discussed how as an individual you should learn to defend, but recall at all times that defending is not just applying these skills to cope with the man you are marking but, very importantly, to help your team-mates in defence. Also, remember that to defend well you will always have to know

- ☐ where the ball is,
- ☐ where your man is, and
- ☐ where you are yourself in relation to the basket.

When you can do this you will have got over a major hurdle in becoming a good defensive player and an important facet of your team's defence. You do not win matches if you play a slack defence.

5 Attack

Once your opposing team has acquired good basic skills and its players are aware of their team responsibilities in defence it will be increasingly difficult for you to score baskets. The frustration of being unable to score generally reflects in the play, which in turn tends to become erratic, with individuals making forced passes and shooting from too far out or when under pressure from a defender.

In order to combat efficient defences a team has to establish a more controlled attacking play. This requires them to establish and understand the areas of responsibility for each player, based on the need to maintain *width* and *depth* in the offensive pattern so as to stretch the defending team at all times and consequently create more space and provide easier passing lanes. Don't at any time be pressurised into forced passes, dribbles or shots.

Initially, it is a good idea to separate the team into 'big' players who are good material for post players and rebounders and 'small' players (called guards) who take up positions further from the basket. The biggest player will probably become a centre or post player, while another big player will have the task of 'running the baseline'. In the nature of things, one of the players will probably stand out at a competent dribbler and good passer of the ball. These skills are needed by the player who will become the playmaker or ball-handler. The remainder of the smaller players will take the other guard positions as described and outlined in the rest of this chapter.

Areas of responsibility

The position the post or centre player takes up often dictates the pattern of play (Figure 45). If, for instance, he stands on the foul line at centre, it would be unusual for the guard to be able to shoot from the head of the key. When he goes into a post position it usually results in the forward being pushed further out towards the side line (Figure 46).

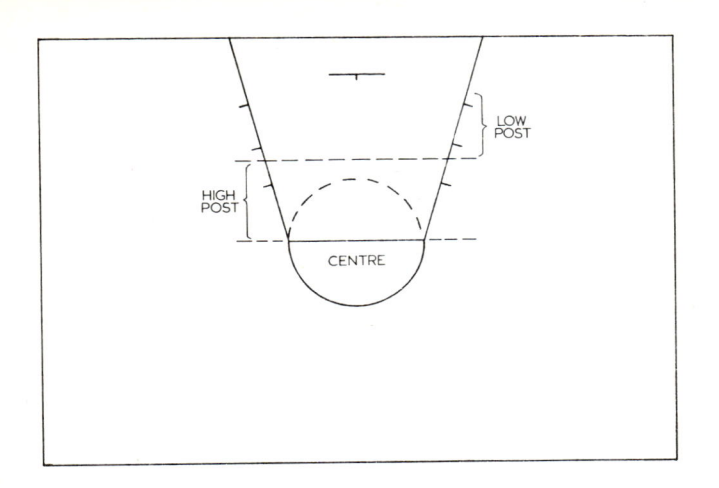

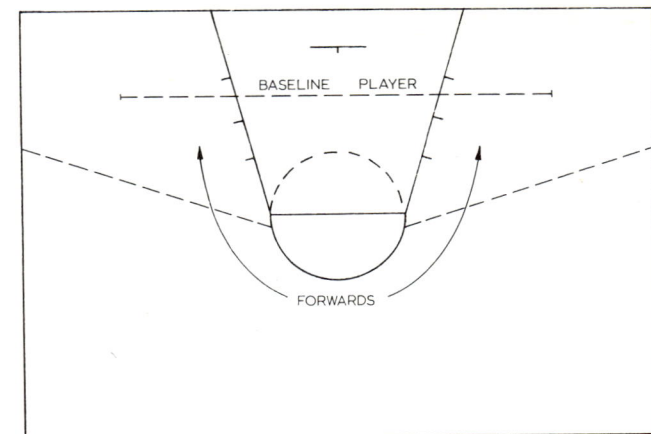

Fig 45

Fig 46

The baseline player has to be able to see the ball all the time. His position is often determined by the presence or absence of the post player; see Figure 46. He is anxious to preserve not only depth around the key but also balance. Quite often, when his team has two players on either side of the key, his aim will be to move across to the other side to create an 'overload'; i.e., three or four players on one side of the court.

Forwards/guards operate in the shaded area, and the depth of their playing area is governed by the presence/absence of the baseline player, while the width is determined by the presence of the post player; see Figures 46 & 47. In the absence of the baseline player the forward may find himself being forced closer to the baseline by the playmaker/guard bringing the ball around to the side. He has to be capable of quick, accurate passes to the baseline and

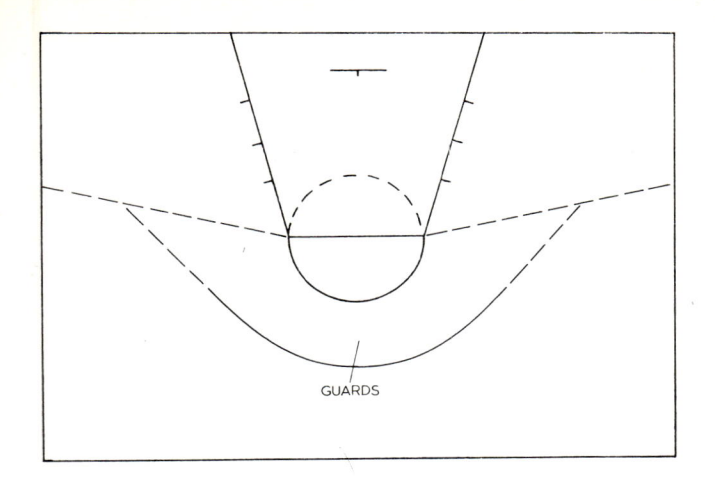

Fig 47

post players and of driving to left or right in order to establish his own shooting position.

The guard seeks to direct play by taking advantage of lapses in defensive marking. He preserves width and depth and encourages ball movement. He attacks gaps, creating shooting opportunities for himself and his team-mates. He moves around with the ball, never passing from one position only. While his main preoccupation is with attack he also has to bear in mind defence, so that should the attack fail then he is in a position to defend against a quick counter-attack.

Plays against a zone defence

Certain general rules should be remembered at all times when attacking:
- PATIENCE;
- move the ball and use the unpressured passing lanes;
- move players;
- attack the gaps;
- only take good shots;
- rebound; and
- PATIENCE again – when one team has the ball, the other team cannot score, so don't throw it away.

You may find that some players want to run everywhere – and all of them running at the same time gives as many problems to the ball-holder as it gives to the defence. It is important, therefore, that each player understands his role and the way that the team aims to create situations from which one player has a good chance to score.

The key to successfully attacking a zone defence depends on players' ability to move the ball around until they find a team-mate in a good shooting position. It is by quick, accurate passing that your team will create a situation where one of your players receives the ball in a position without pressure from a defender and from where he can get in an easy shot. Here are some methods by which a team may achieve this.

Attacking the gaps
If the other team play a typical 2–1–2 zone defence then your team may well play a 1–3–1 offence, so that from the outset you attack the gaps. Figure 48 shows the playmaker X1 with three options. He can feed X3 or can dribble or pass to X2 or X4, who may then be free to shoot. If X3 receives the ball, he can now shoot, if he is free, or pass to X2 or X4 who can then shoot. X5 can also cut in from the baseline to receive a pass from X3 for a shot – and so on. It is quick passing and movement of this type which enable a team to attack the gaps inherent in any system of defence. It will not, however, be easy, and your team will have to work hard for each other in order to create situations where one member is free to receive the ball and to get in an easy shot.

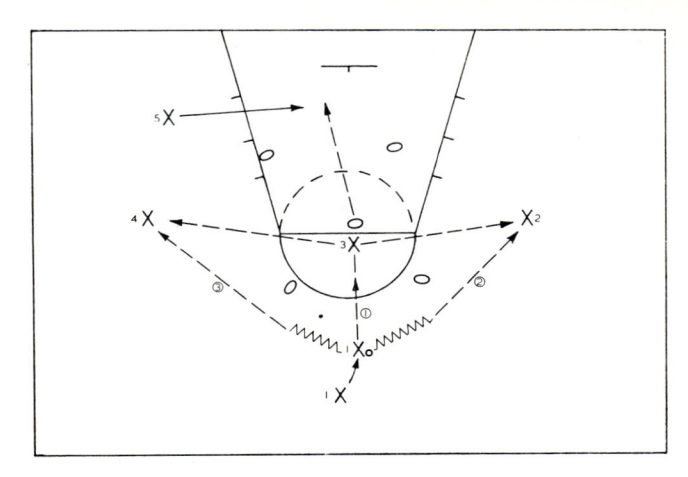

Fig 48

Principles of an overload
Figure 49 shows what happens to the zone when the offensive team moves its players onto one side of the court. When this 'overload' occurs the defensive team must shift to combat it. X1 can now attack the gap and can then either shoot or pass to X2, X3 or X4. Each of these players may have a shot or can in turn pass. If X3 receives the ball he can pass to X5, who either moves out for a pass or cuts in toward the

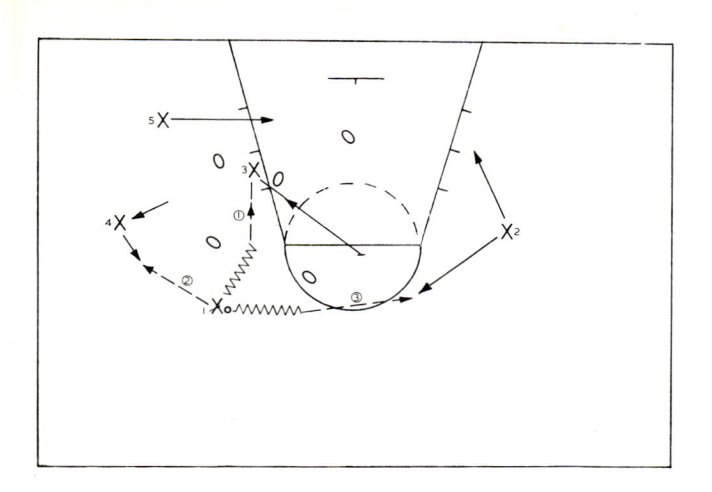

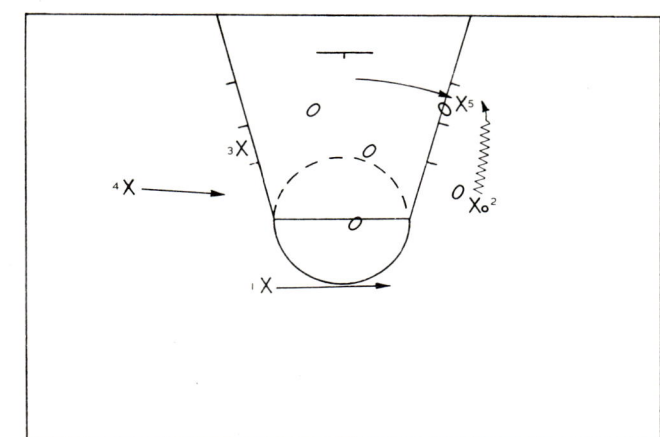

Fig 49

Fig 50

basket. X1 may, however, dribble and pass to X4 or X2, who have been left comparatively free.

Figure 50 shows what is likely to happen if X2 receives the ball and is unable to get in a shot. Assuming that X5 has come across the baseline, X2 can now dribble to the baseline and shoot over X5. He can pass to X5 and cut to the baseline for a return pass and a shot, or he can pass out to X1.

The process of passing the ball, attacking the gaps and moving players is repeated until you have got one of your players in a good shooting position with time to take his shot. Always be ready to go back to the beginning and start again – 30 seconds is a long time.

Plays against a man-to-man defence

Each player by this time will have acquired some individual skills in dribbling, passing and shooting.

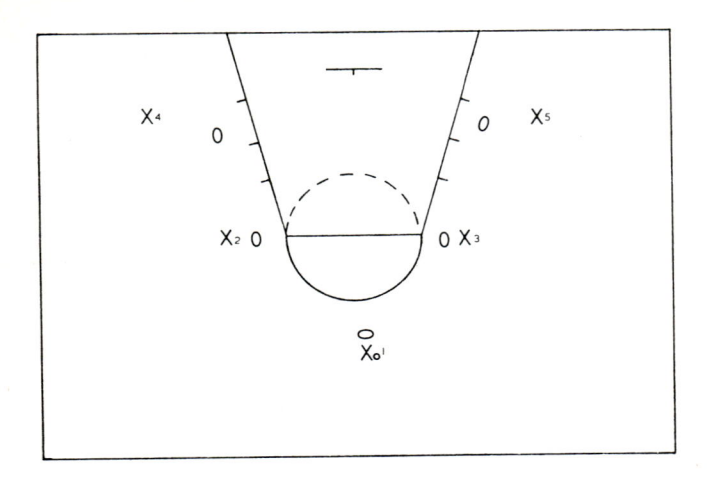

Fig 51

These skills enable the team to overcome a man-to-man defence.

Certain rules should be remembered at all times when confronted by a man-to-man defence:
- PATIENCE;
- quick ball movement – use the unpressured passing lanes;
- decisive dribbling – go hard to the boards;
- player movement;
- good screens;
- keep your head up – be able to see all round;
- only take good shots; and
- PATIENCE again – when a team has the ball its opponents cannot score, so don't throw it away.

Once again the critical aspects are balance in attack and using players to maintain width and depth. A team can, of course, design its own pattern of attack to create a situation in which a player has a one-on-one play, simply by players moving from one side of the keyway to the other thus leaving a team-mate with the ball and his defender so that he has a one-on-one situation. However, some tried and tested team plays against a man-to-man defence are described here.

1–2–2 offence against a man-to-man defence

The vital positions are shown in Figure 51. X1 has the ball. Some of the alternative plays which may be used are outlined below. In each instance the play can be performed on both sides of the basket.
- X1 can fake a pass and if his defender falls off can shoot.
- X1 passes to X2, fakes to screen X3 and cuts for basket to receive the ball and score.
- X1 passes to X2 and screens X2, who now uses

the screen to dribble for a jump shot.

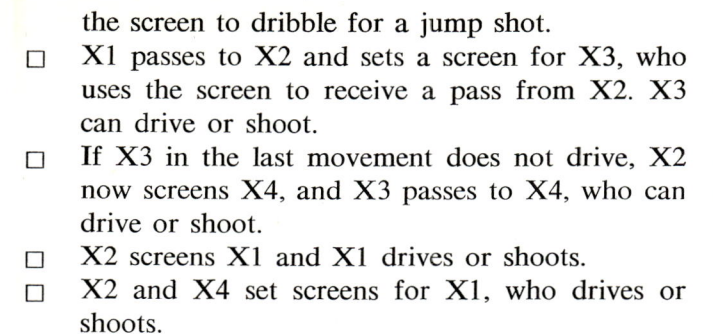

- [ ] X1 passes to X2 and sets a screen for X3, who uses the screen to receive a pass from X2. X3 can drive or shoot.
- [ ] If X3 in the last movement does not drive, X2 now screens X4, and X3 passes to X4, who can drive or shoot.
- [ ] X2 screens X1 and X1 drives or shoots.
- [ ] X2 and X4 set screens for X1, who drives or shoots.
- [ ] X4 screens for X5 as X1 passes to X2. X2 then passes to X5 who can drive or shoot.

There are other options, all based on this simple play. The important rule is patience – only shoot the easy, unpressurised shots. The team has to be prepared to pass and screen many times before a good scoring opportunity is made. When a shot is made, all players but X1 should rebound.

So far we have explained some basic individual and team skills which are essential in order to play basketball well. However, the only way to acquire these skills is through practice. The next chapter is devoted to this aspect.

6 Team Practice

Practice is a very important part of developing both a player's individual and team skills. This chapter discusses some of the drills and other practices which can be used. Remember, the more a player practises, the greater the level of skill that he will develop.

Before the practice starts

There are many clubs throughout the country where players arrive for practice perhaps an hour early. Quite often their pre-practice routine consists of simply throwing the ball at the basket. Naturally, the whole aim of the game is to score baskets, and this aspect must not be overlooked. Similarly it should not be overemphasised. A person by himself can practise passing, dribbling, shooting and rebounding, and with a team-mate can play one against one. Three people can play 2 *v* 1; four 2 *v* 2 and so on. Here are some simple basketball drills which can be used when numbers are short.

Follow the leader
One ball for each player and follow the leader. Whatever that player does, the others do. If the leader dribbles left-handed, jump shoots, passes the ball against the wall or rebounds the ball off the backboard, then the others follow suit. After two minutes the second player should take over as 'leader', then the third, and so on.

One against one
In this practice, the players simulate real game conditions in the following way:

- ☐ The players involved shoot free-throws to decide who goes first.
- ☐ The player defending hands the ball to the attacker in any position which the attacker takes up outside the three-second area.
- ☐ When the attacker has the ball he is allowed to shoot or to dribble in accord with the rules of

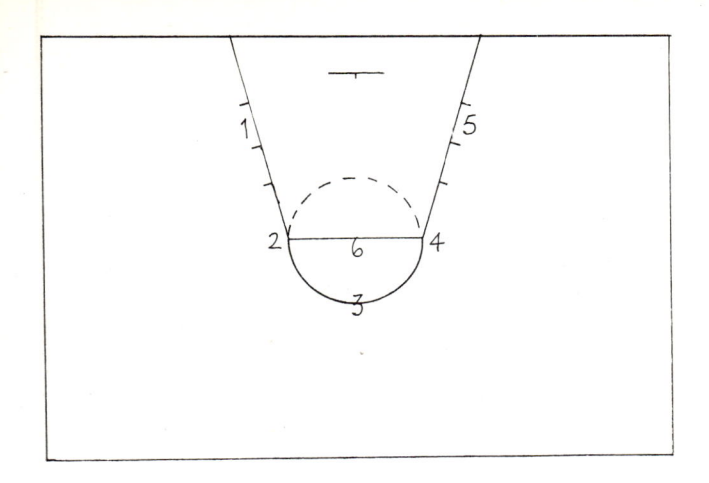

Fig 52

the game. When the attacker has shot, both players may rebound. If the attacker gains the rebound he can shoot or dribble again from where he gets the ball.
- [ ] If the attacker scores then he is allowed to take the ball again.
- [ ] When the defender gets the ball it is his chance to score in the same way.

The first player to get (say) five baskets wins, or the player to score most baskets out of five possessions wins.

Two against two, three against three, etc., are all played on the same principle, but the team-mates can now pass and screen as in the game itself. Similar scoring is used to that outlined above.

Round the world

This is good pre-practice shooting drill for two or more players. One player shoots from several agreed positions on court and continues to shoot until he misses. Then it is the turn of the next player, and so on. Typical points to shoot from are shown in Figure 52. The first player to score from all six points wins.

The practice sessions

How long and how often the team has practice sessions will vary. Obviously, the longer the sessions and the more frequently they take place, the more effective they will be.

Principally, the practice session is the opportunity for a team to develop the players' individual and team skills required in the game itself. It is important, therefore, to allocate the available time to the tasks on hand. A suggestion is to follow these time allocations.

Type of practice	Approximate % of time
Individual skills	50
Team plays (defence and attack)	35
Scrimmage game	15

The above breakdown is only a guide, but it is most important to spend a substantial amount of time in any practice night improving the individual skills of players. Until players have acquired the necessary skills their ability to play well within a team is limited.

Also, it is often best to follow the above pattern for the evening itself, starting with individual skills and finishing the sessions with a scrimmage game between the players so that they can put into practice some of the individual and team skills they have worked on earlier.

This chapter concentrates on describing the ways in which individual skills can be developed. The chapters on team defence and attack will help to formulate which methods of defence and attack the team uses, and during the time spent on practice these methods should be discussed and practised.

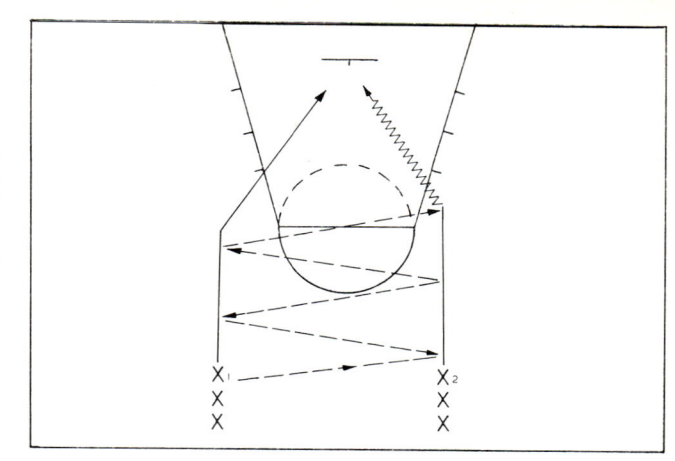

Fig 53

Individual skills

Many of these have been described and discussed in earlier chapters. Here is a set of drills which are designed to concentrate a player's practice on developing certain specific skills which he will need as either an attacker or a defender. Each drill is described, and it is important to concentrate on all the skills involved in order to complete the drill correctly.

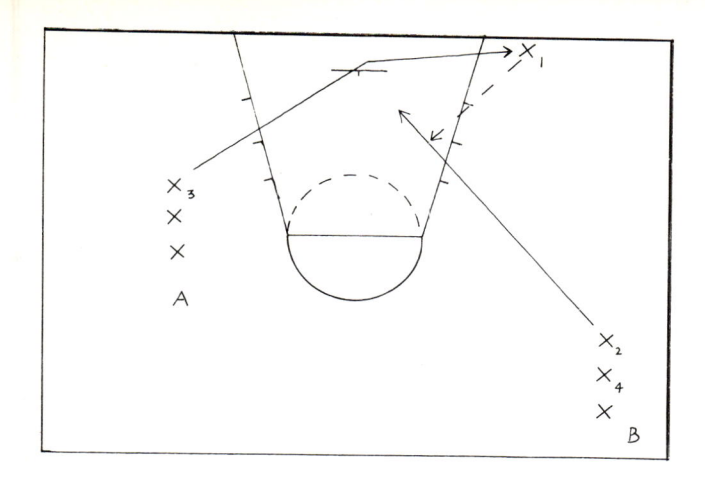

Fig 54

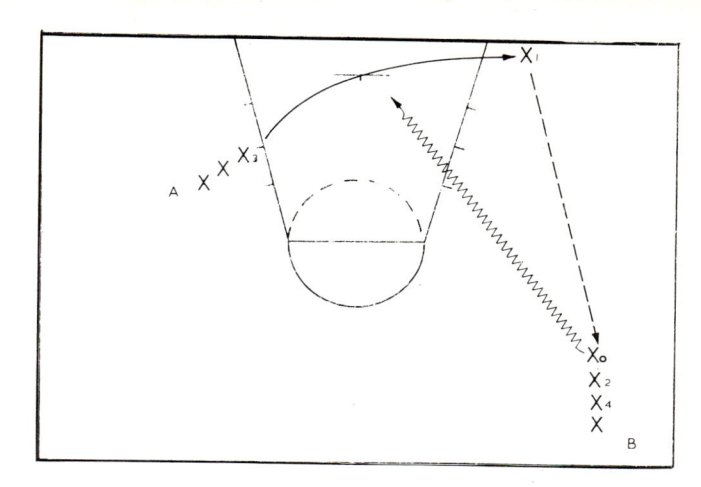

Fig 55

Shooting drills

Lay-up drills

X1 and X2 interpass until they reach the keyway. X2 now drives in for a lay-up. X1 follows in to rebound (Figure 53).

X2 runs straight towards the basket. X1 passes the ball so that X2 does not have to bounce the ball before taking his lay-up. X1 joins column A. X2 joins column B. X3 rebounds as X4 runs in and receives a pass from X3 (Figure 54).

X1 passes to X2. X2 dribbles in for a lay-up. X1 joins column A. X2 joins column B. X3 rebounds passes to X4. X4 dribbles in for a lay-up (Figure 55).

X1 stands on the foul line in the corner. X2 provides a 'passive' defence. X1 fakes left and takes a one bounce drive and lay-up to the basket. X2 and X1 rebound. X2 joins column B. X1 joins column A.

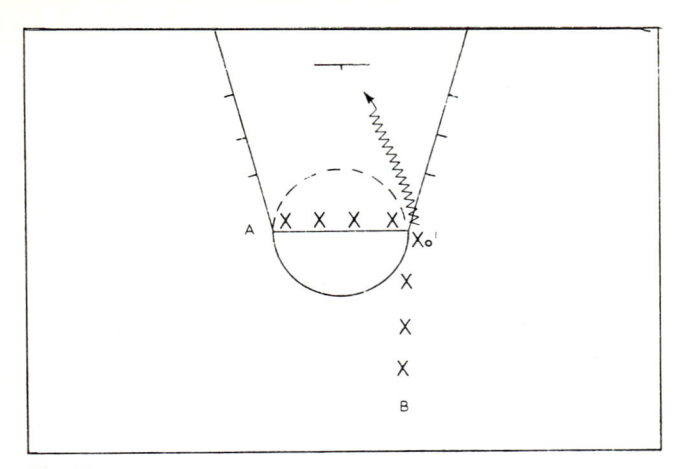

Fig 56

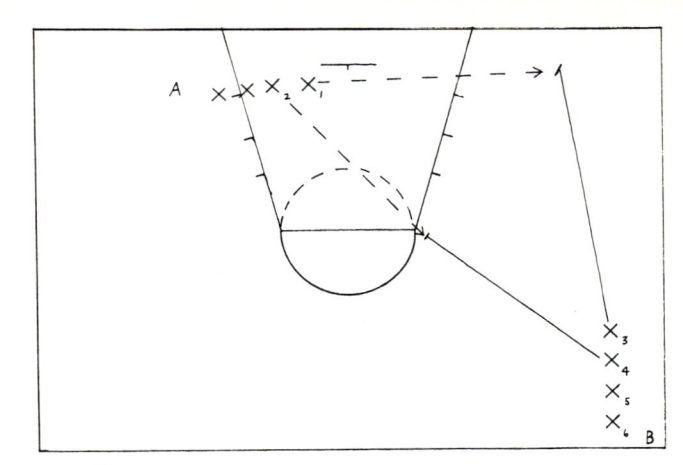

Fig 57

These drills should also be performed from the left-hand side.

Jump-shot drills

X3 cuts to the baseline. X1 passes to X3 who takes a jump shot. X4 cuts to the head of the keyway. X2 passes to X4 who takes a jump shot. X1 and X2 join column B. X3 and X4 join column A (Figure 56).

X1 feeds ball to the centre who passes off to the cutting player X2. X2 receives and passes immediately to X3 who is cutting to the basket. X3 shoots a jump shot. X1 follows the ball and becomes centre player. X2 rebounds the ball, feeds X1 column and joins X3 column. X3 shoots and joins X1 column. X5 joins X2 column. When it is running smoothly introduce another basketball.

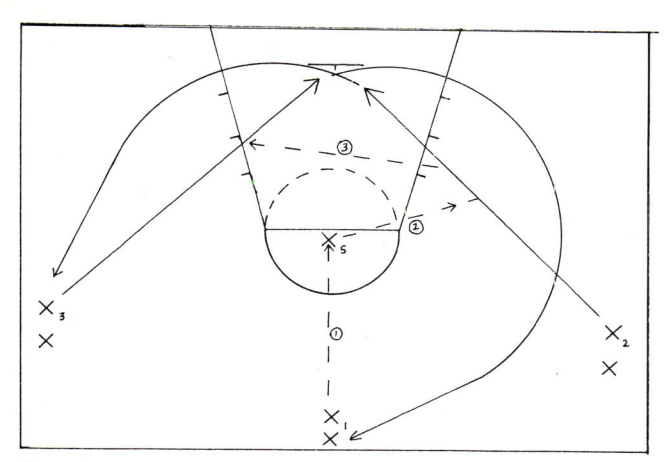

Fig 58

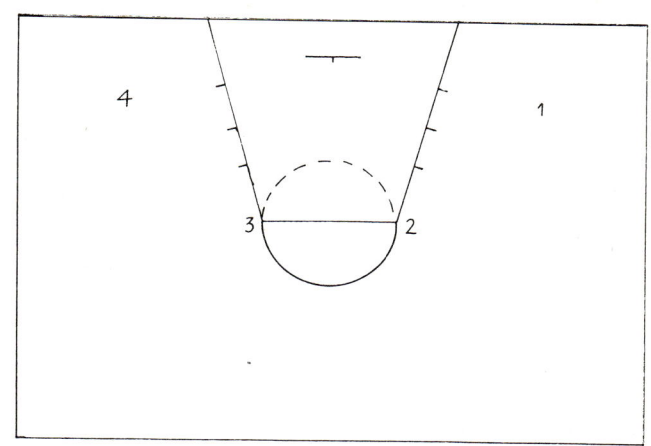

Fig 59

Set-shot drill

The aim of this drill is for one team to score twenty-one points before another team, as follows. Two teams are at each basket with one team shooting from position 1 and the other from position 4 (see Figure 59). The first player, in his own time, shoots – if he scores he gets two points. Whether he scores or not, if he can rebound the ball before it touches the floor he is allowed to shoot again, but only once – if he scores this time he gets one point. After his try, the player rebounds and passes to his next team-mate. When the first team scores twenty-one points they win that round and both teams immediately move to points 2 and 3 respectively, and so on through all four positions.

If both teams win two rounds each they play-off immediately from positions 2 and 3 respectively. This can then be followed, if a number of teams are involved, by the winners and losers playing off for final positions in the competition.

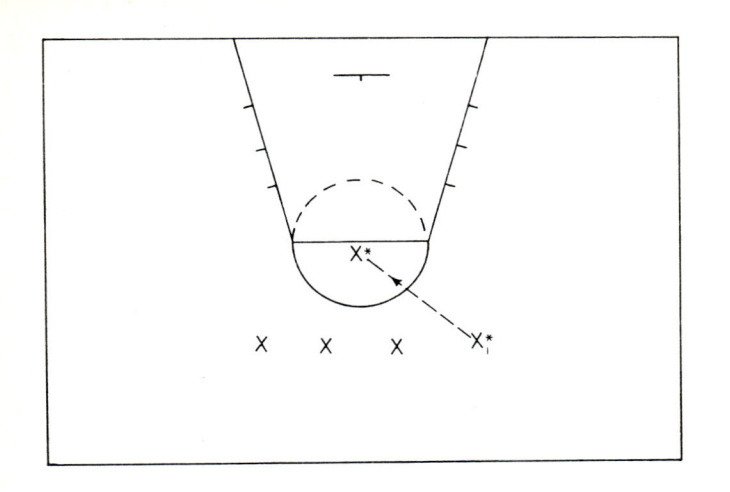

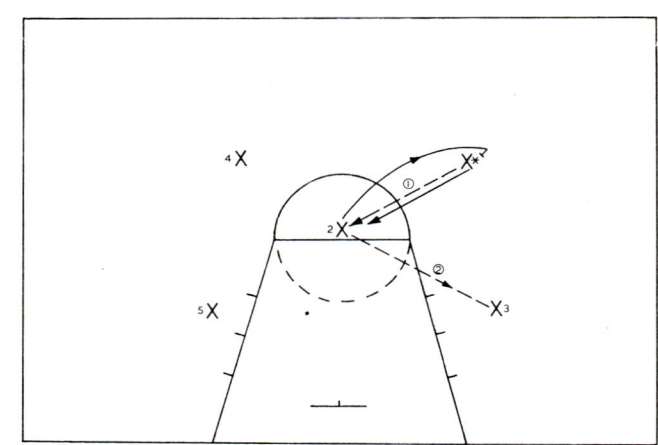

Fig 60

Fig 61

Passing drills

Pepperpot

Players starred in Figure 60 start with a basketball. X1* starts by chest-passing the ball to X*. As soon as the ball is on its way X* passes to any other X, catches the ball from X1* and waits until the ball is thrown again from X. Do not fake a pass but keep the ball moving quickly.

Rosso drill

X* starts the passing into the centre and follows the ball. X2 receives, passes to X3 and takes the place of X*. X3 passes to the centre and follows the ball. X* receives, passes off to X4 and takes the place of X3. X4 receives, passes to the centre and follows the ball. X3 receives, passes to X5 and takes the place of X4. The drill should be walked through at first and the

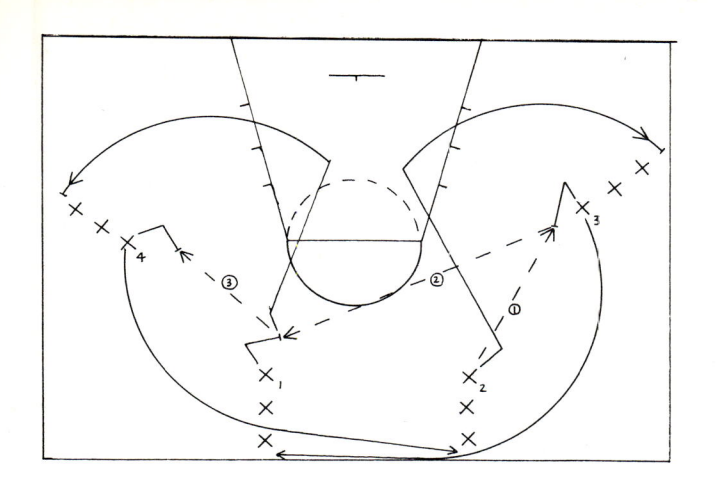

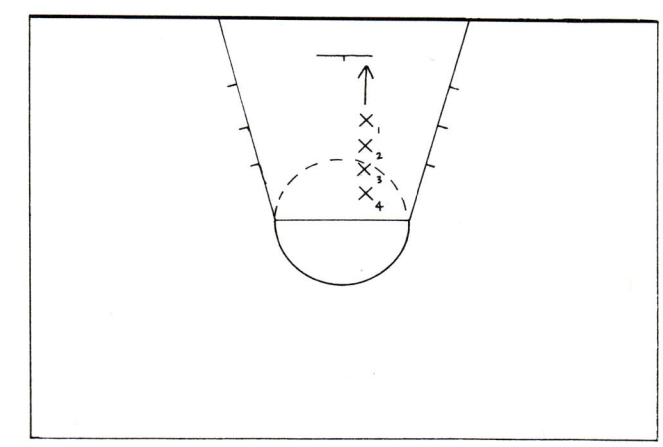

Fig 62

Fig 63

tempo increased as the players get used to the movements involved (Figure 61).

Four men continuity with one basketball

Guard X2 passes to forward X3, cuts and replaces him. X3 passes back to centre after faking a pass to cutter. He then joins the end of the opposite line. Guard X1 steps up, moves in to meet the pass from X3, passes to forward X4, cuts and replaces X4. X4 fakes a pass to cutter and passes ball back into the centre and joins the end of the opposite line. X3 steps in to meet the pass and the drill continues (Figure 62).

Rebounding drill

X1 has the ball and throws it high onto the backboard. X2 follows behind X1 and taps the ball back

77

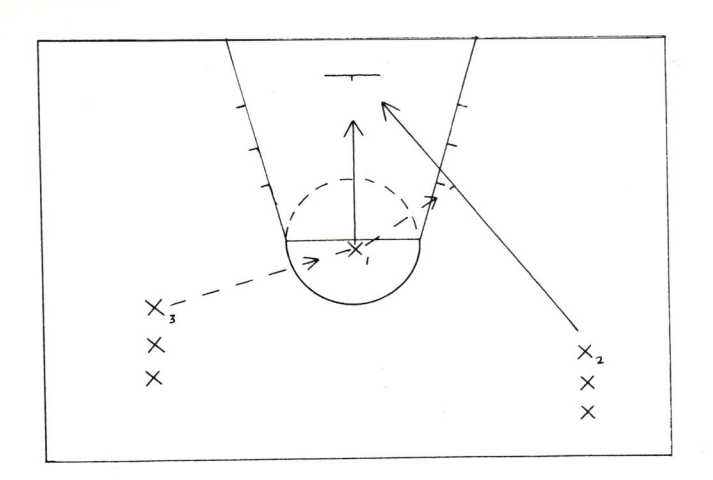

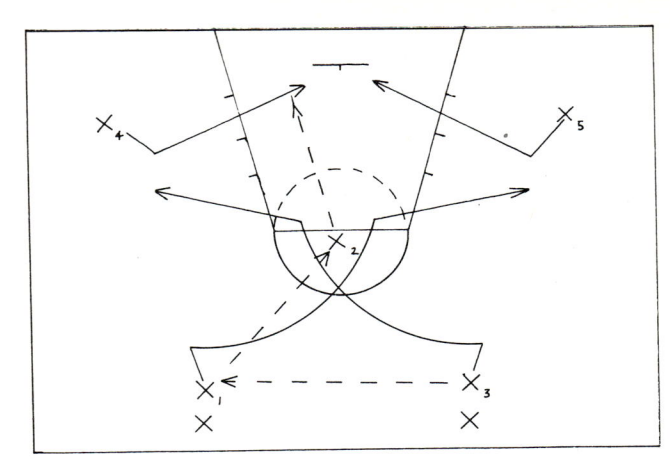

Fig 64

Fig 65

up onto the backboard. X3 follows X2, and so on. Following the tap each player rejoins the end of the column (Figure 63).

Cutting drills

X3 passes to X1, who passes off to the cutting player X2. X2 takes his lay-up and X1 rebounds. If the basket is scored, X1 passes to X3 and the drill repeats. If X2 does not score, X1 rebounds and scores, then passes out to X3. X3 takes place of X1, X2 joins X3 column, and X1 joins X2 column (Figure 64).

Split the post – no shooting

Guard X3 passes to Guard X1, who passes to centre X2 (the post).

Guards cut either side of X2 (split the post) and move out to take the forwards' place. Forwards X4 and X5 fake and cut to the basket to receive from X2. Forwards now replace the guards.

This can alternatively be used as a shooting drill with the non shooting forward, rebounding and passing the ball to the guards.

These are a few of the many drills which you can use in a practice session. To be effective, we consider that drills should be enjoyable and not complicated – remember that the drill is intended to improve a player's individual skills and to simulate game situations; it should, therefore, be easy to understand, with the concentration being centred, rather than on the rules of the drill, on the individual skills contained within it – the correct footwork, dribbling and shooting hand, shooting technique, timing, rebounding, passing, receiving and so on. Practising hard on good techniques will bring a high level of skill, and that achievement will bring you success in basketball.

7 Mini-Basketball

The points we have already made about the game of basketball, the development of a team and the skills and techniques to be learned, are relevant to all age groups. But during the last few years mini-basketball has spread throughout UK schools. This game is of particular relevance now that we have middle schools for 8–12 year olds, for mini-basketball is intended for girls and boys under the age of 13. In order not to repeat ourselves unnecessarily, we have included only the rules of mini-basketball, which differ in many respects from those of the major game.

Rule No. 1

Definition of the game
Art. 1
   Mini-basketball is a game, based on basketball, for girls and boys under 13 years of age on September 1st of the school year.

Aim of the game
   A mini-basketball match is played by two teams of five players each.
   The aim of each team is to throw the ball into the opponents' basket and to stop the opposing team from getting the ball or scoring within the rules of the game.

Rule No. 2

Facilities and materials

The court
Art. 3
   The size of court is:
   Length 26 metres
   Width 14 metres

Other measurements can be used, providing they are in the same proportion to one another. (Most courts are approximately 18 metres long by 10.5 metres wide.)

Lines
Art. 4

The lines of a mini-basketball court are the same as those drawn on a regular basketball court.
These are:
- the side and endlines;
- the centre circle;
- the zone lines; and
- the free-throw lines.

The free-throw lines must always be drawn exactly four metres from the backboards.

Backboards and baskets
Art. 5

The backboards are placed at both ends of the court, parallel to the endlines, with their lower edge 2.35 metres above the ground.
The size of backboards is:
Height 0.90 metres
Width 1.20 metres

The baskets have the following measurements:
Height 2.60 metres above the ground
Diameter 0.45 metres
Nets 0.40 metres long

The ball
Art. 6

It must be spherical and it can be covered with leather, synthetic material or rubber.
Circumference 0.68 to 0.78 metres
Weight 450 to 500 grams

Rule No. 3

The teams

Team
Art. 7

Each team is made up of ten players:
- five players on the court; and
- five substitutes.

The coach
Art. 8

The coach is the leader of the team. He gives advice to his players at the court side. He

81

arranges players' substitutions. He is assisted by the team captain.

Clothing
Art. 9

The players of each team must wear shirts of the same colour and every player wears a number on the front and back of this shirt.

Rule No. 4

The officials

The referee
Art. 10

He officiates in the games. He calls violations and fouls. He awards or cancels baskets when they are made. He administers penalties according to the rules.

The scorekeeper
Art. 11

He keeps the scoresheet, on which he puts down, opposite the names and numbers of the players of both teams, the points they score and the fouls the referee calls on them.

The timekeeper
Art. 12

He controls the playing time and notifies the referee at the end of each period.

Rule No. 5

The match

Time in play
Art. 13

The match is divided into *two halves of twenty minutes each,* with a *ten-minute interval* between them. Each half is divided into *two periods of ten minutes each*, with a compulsory interval of *two minutes* between them.

The timekeeper controls the time in play without stopping the clock, except in those exceptional cases decided by the referee.

Scoring
Art. 14

Basket made 2 points
Free throw made 1 point
The final result may show a winner or a tie between the two teams.

Rule No. 6

Players' Substitution
Art. 15

Each member of the team must play at least one 10-minute period.

During the first three periods, substitutions can only take place during an interval. During these first three periods each of the ten players of a team must have played in the match for at least one period but not more than two. During the fourth period, one *time out* of one minute may be granted to each of the teams, upon a request by the coach. During these time outs both coaches may substitute players.

Rule No. 7

Technical rules

How to play with the ball
Art. 16

In mini-basketball, as in basketball, the *ball is held and played with the hands*. It may be passed, shot or dribbled in any direction, within the limits of the rules of the game. To strike the ball with the fist or the foot is a violation.

Ball out-of-bounds
Art. 17

The ball is out-of-bounds
- ☐ when it touches the floor, or any person or object situated outside the court or on the boundary lines;
- ☐ when it touches a player who is himself outside the court or on the boundary lines; or
- ☐ when it hits the support or the back of the backboard.

If a ball is put out-of-bounds by two opponents or if the referee is in doubt as to who caused the out-of-bounds, the referee will declare a jump ball.

Progression with the ball
Art. 18

A player may not move while carrying the ball.

A player who holds the ball can only take *two steps* on the ground and must get rid of it before executing a third step.

Art. 19

A player who receives the ball when standing still, or stops correctly after catching it, *is allowed to pivot*. 'Pivoting' means moving one foot in any direction whilst the other remains in contact with the ground.

Art. 20

When a player wants to advance with the ball, *he may dribble*, that is bounce the ball to the ground with one hand.

The player is forbidden to
- [ ] dribble with two hands at the same time;
- [ ] allow the ball to rest in one hand while dribbling; or to
- [ ] dribble again after the ball comes to rest in his hands.

Three-second rule
Art. 21

A player is forbidden to remain *longer than three seconds* in the opponents' 'restricted area' when his team has possession of the ball. The 'restricted area' is the floor limited by the end line, the free throw line and the two zone lines. The lines form part of the 'restricted area'.

Five-second rule
Art. 22

A player who passes the ball into play from the sideline, following a violation committed by the opponents, or from the end line, following a basket scored by an opponent, has *five seconds to put the ball in play*. The time is counted from the moment the ball is in the player's hands.

A closely guarded player may not keep the ball *more than five seconds*; if he does, the referee will call a jump ball.

The player who is to take a free throw has *five-seconds* to take his shot. The time is counted from the moment the ball has been given to the player by the referee on the free-throw line.

Thirty-second rule
Art. 23

When a team has possession of the ball, it must take a shot at the basket *within thirty seconds*. If the ball goes out-of-bounds during the thirty seconds and the same team keeps possession, a new thirty-second period begins.

Rule No. 8

Violations and sanctions
Art. 24

A *violation* is the breaking of the 'technical rules' set out in Rule No. 7. When there is a violation, the referee should call it, and the ball becomes 'dead' the moment the referee blows his whistle. Generally, after a violation, the ball is put in play by an opponent of the player who committed the violation. The pass from out-of-bounds is always on the sideline, at the spot indicated by the referee, that is near the spot, on the court where the violation happened.

Passes
Art. 25

The player putting the ball into play must stay outside the court, behind the sideline, at the spot indicated by the referee. On the court, where there is very little space behind the line, no other player should be nearer than *one metre* to the player passing the ball into court.

Jump ball
Art. 26

A jump ball takes place in the following cases:
- *centre jump* at the beginning of every period;
- *held ball*, that is when two opponents hold the ball at the same time or when a closely guarded player holds the ball for five seconds;
- *out-of-bounds ball*, caused by two opponents, or where the referee is uncertain;
- *ball lodges in the basket supports;*
- *double foul* (see further on).

The referee tosses the ball vertically between the two players concerned. They can tap the ball after it has reached the peak of its upward throw.

The jump ball is held:
- *in the centre circle* (always at beginning of periods); or
- *in one of the free throw circles* depending where the violation was committed.

85

Rule No. 9

Behaviour rules

The spirit of the game
Art. 27

In mini-basketball, as in basketball, the players should always show *the best spirit of co-operation and sportsmanship. All those players who act deliberately in an unsportsmanlike manner must be expelled from the game.*

Mini-basketball, like basketball, is a *non-contact game.* Players, either when defending or attacking, should make every effort to avoid contact with their opponents.

One should never forget that the opponent is a playmate.

Rules on contact

GENERAL RULE
Art. 28

When contact occurs between two opponents, it is the referee's duty to decide who was to blame for this contact, and to decide whether the contact was intentional or not, and to administer the proper penalty. Accidental contact that has no bearing on the normal course of the game can be ignored.

RESPONSIBILITY OF CONTACT
Art. 29

The referee will blame the player who has caused the contact or has not attempted to avoid it. The player who is to blame for the contact commits a personal foul.

Principal personal fouls

DEFENSIVE FOULS
Art. 30

Obstruction consists of stopping or slowing down movement of a player who is not in possession of the ball with the extended arms, or the hips and knees.

Holding consists of reducing an opponent's freedom of movement.

Pushing consists, particularly, of causing contact by approaching an opponent from behind.

Hacking consists of making any sort of contact with the opponent, in attempting to stop his progression.

OFFENSIVE FOULS
Art. 31

Charging is the type of contact caused by the forward movement of a player who has just taken a shot at the basket and does not try to avoid the opponent. *The charging drive* consists of the dribbler contacting an opponent standing in his path or trying to drive between two defenders when he has no room to do so.

Fouls and their penalties
Art. 32

A *personal foul* is a breaking of the rules by a player who causes contact with an opponent. When there is a personal foul, the referee must blow his whistle and take hold of the ball. In each case, the referee:
- ☐ indicates to the scorekeeper the number of the guilty player, so that a 'personal foul' can be marked on the score sheet against the player; and
- ☐ then proceeds to administer the penalty (see further on).

If two opponents at the same time commit a foul on each other, there is a *double foul*. The referee then calls a personal foul on each of the guilty players, and play is resumed with a jump ball.

Classification of fouls

SIMPLE (OR 'NORMAL') FOUL
Art. 33

This is a personal foul that is committed by a player who makes contact with the opponent accidentally.

INTENTIONAL FOUL
Art. 34

This is a personal foul that is committed by a player who *deliberately* makes contact with an opponent, with the purpose of preventing him from playing normally. A foul that is committed on a player when he is taking a shot at the basket is always considered as being intentional.

DISQUALIFYING FOUL
Art. 35

This is a blatant, unsportsmanlike foul, committed by a player on an opponent with the deliberate intention to contact him roughly.

DOUBLE FOUL

Art. 36

A double foul is a situation in which two opponents commit a foul on each other at approximately the same time.

MULTIPLE FOUL

Art. 37

A multiple foul is a situation in which two or more members of one team commit personal fouls on the same opponent at approximately the same time.

PENALTIES APPLIED TO GUILTY PLAYERS

Art. 38

In every case a personal foul is marked by the score-keeper on the score sheet opposite the name of the guilty player, in the 'fouls' column by entering the time (in full minutes) when the foul took place.

In the case of a disqualifying foul he shall add a capital D.

FIFTH FOUL

Art. 39

A player who commits his fifth personal foul is automatically expelled from the game by the referee. A substitute may take his place.

DISQUALIFYING FOUL

Art. 40

A player who commits a disqualifying foul is immediately expelled from the game by the referee. A substitute may take his place.

Awards to the opponents

IN THE CASE OF A NORMAL FOUL

Art. 41

The referee gives the ball to any one of the guilty player's opponents, in order that he may put the ball into play from the sideline from a spot opposite to the spot where the foul was committed.

IN THE CASE OF A DOUBLE FOUL

Art. 43

No free throw is awarded, and play is restarted with a jump ball between the two guilty players.

IN THE CASE OF A MULTIPLE FOUL

Art. 44

When two or more personal fouls are committed on a player by opponents the player who was fouled is awarded two free throws, whatever the number of fouls committed on him. No free throw is awarded if, at the moment the foul was committed the player who was fouled was shooting and scores.

The free throw

THE WAY A FREE THROW SHOULD BE TAKEN
Art. 45

The shooter stands behind the free throw line and receives the ball from the referee. He must take his shot within five seconds.

The other players can stand in the spaces marked along the zone lines:
- ☐ two defenders in the spaces nearest to the basket; and
- ☐ two attackers in the other two spaces.

No player can enter the three-second zone before the ball has touched the rim.

VIOLATIONS AND SANCTIONS

By the shooter: no point can be counted and an out-of-bounds ball from the sideline is awarded to the opponents.

By a defender: the basket counts if the ball has gone in; otherwise another attempt is awarded to the shooter.

By one of the shooter's team-mates: the basket counts if the ball has gone in; otherwise, an out-of-bounds ball from the sideline is awarded to the opponents.

Officiating

Girls and boys can also referee, coach, score and timekeep. They should try to help all the players to enjoy a fair and good game.

The referee should be a 'friend' assisting everyone to understand the game. He should not be too severe. Remember beginners will learn best by being told where they made mistakes.

All mini-basketball enquiries in the UK should be addressed to

Kenneth G. Charles,
Headmaster,
The Greneway School,
Garden Walk,
Royston, Herts. SE8 7JF.

Glossary

Knowledge of the terms given here will increase your understanding of the game and help explain expressions and phrases used in the text. These terms have been built up over many years and constitute an international language among basketball players. We have tried to limit this glossary to those most commonly used.

AIR DRIBBLE: throwing or tapping the ball into the air and then touching it before it hits the floor.
ALIVE: term used of an offensive player who has the ball, but has not dribbled.
ARC: the trajectory of the ball in flight.
ASSIST: a pass to a team-mate that results in an immediate score.
BACKBOARD: the board supporting the baskets at either end of the court.
BACKCOURT: that half of the court which includes the basket a team is defending. Once a team acquires possession of the ball it is allowed 10 seconds to get the ball from the backcourt to its forecourt. Once in the forecourt the team cannot pass the ball back into its backcourt.
BACKDOOR: term used to describe a cut by an offensive player towards the basket and going to that side of the defensive player away from the ball. It is used mainly when the offensive player is being overplayed or when the defence turns to look at the ball or in another direction.
BACK-IN: this occurs when a pivotman is moving backwards towards the basket, with or without the ball, and he makes contact with a defender. A foul should be called on the pivotman.
BACK-TAP: this occurs when a player involved in a jump ball taps the ball back towards the basket his team is defending.
BALL CONTROL GAME: a type of offensive play that emphasises maintaining possession of the ball until a good shot is possible.
BALL HAWK: a player who is adept in recovering the ball either by intercepting a pass or by snapping up a loose ball.

91

BANK SHOT: a ball shot onto the backboard so that it rebounds into the basket.

BASELINE DRIVE: a drive made close to the offensive end line of the court.

BLOCKING OUT: the positioning of the defensive player in such a manner as to prevent an offensive player from moving to the basket to gain a rebound.

BOX AND ONE: a term used to describe a combination defence with four men playing a zone defence in a square formation (i.e., 2:2) and one man out chasing or marking a particular opponent. You can also use a 'Diamond and one'.

BREAK: the rapid movement of a player to a position where he hopes to receive a pass.

BRUSH-OFF (brush off screen): to cause one's opponent to run into a third player thus 'losing' him momentarily.

BUTTONHOOK: to move in one direction, turn sharply and double back.

CENTRE: the name of one of the positions of the team, usually that of the tallest player in the team – the *post player* (q.v.).

CHARGING: a personal foul caused by a player making bodily contact by running into an opponent. Usually committed by an offensive player.

CHASER: in a zone defence, the front player who follows the ball, pressuring the offensive player who has possession.

CHECK: to stop an opponent, usually when shooting, without physical contact.

CIRCULATION: a player's movements about the court on offence.

CLEAR OUT: an offensive manoeuvre in which players vacate an area of court so as to isolate one offensive player and one defensive player. The offensive player may then attempt to score against his opponent who has no defensive team-mates close enough to help him —a one-on-one situation.

CLEAR THE BOARDS: taking a rebound.

CLUTCH SHOOTER: a player who can score when the pressure is on.

COMBINATION DEFENCE: a team defence where some of the team play zone defence and others man-to-man defence.

CONTACT: touching an opponent.

CONTINUITY PLAY: a team offensive system in which men move to one position and then another in a regular order, executing pre-planned play options in an endeavour to create a scoring opportunity. The offensive players' movements on court are so planned that it is not necessary to set up the offensive pattern after each play option has been attempted. The positioning of players after one play option has been attempted is used as the starting position for the next option.

CONTROL BASKETBALL (possession basketball): a style of play in which a team deliberately makes sure of every pass and only shoots when there is a very high percentage chance of scoring.

CONTROLLING THE BOARDS: gaining the majority of the rebounds.

CORNER MAN: a player who stays near the corners to be able to receive a pass for a shot from the man in the middle.

CROSS-COURT PASS: any pass thrown laterally, from one sideline to the other. This pass is easy to intercept.

CROSSOVER: a step used by an offensive player in changing direction, particularly in dribbling, where one foot crosses the other.

CUT: a quick movement by an offensive player without the ball to gain an advantage over the defence; usually directed towards the basket.

CUTTER: a player who cuts or breaks.

CUTAWAY: a player's move in cutting for basket after setting up a screen.

DEAD: describes an offensive player who has used his dribble.

DEFENSIVE BOARD: the backboard that a team is defending.

DOUBLE SCREENS (stack): the situation where two offensive players move between a team-mate and his opponent to block the defensive man.

DOUBLE TEAM: when two defensive players mark one opponent with the ball, usually a temporary measure. (see *trap*).

DRILL: a repetitive practice designed to improve one or more particular fundamental skills or team combinations.

DRIVE: the movement of an offensive player while aggressively moving towards the basket in an attempt to score.

DUNK: a shot in which a jumping player puts the ball down into the opponent's basket from above.

FAKE (feint): a movement made with the aim of deceiving an opponent.

FALL-AWAY: a method of performing certain shots and passes in which the player with the ball moves in one direction as the ball moves in another.

FAST-BREAK: a fast offence that attempts to advance the ball to the front court before the defence is organised, with the object of achieving numerical superiority to give a good shot.

FEED: to pass the ball to a team-mate who is in a scoring position.

FEINT: see *fake*.

FLOATING: a manoeuvre in man-to-man defence where a defender marking an opponent on the weak side stays between his opponent and the basket, but, because the ball is on the opposite side of the court, moves laterally towards it.

FLOOR-PLAY: used to describe the movements on the court of players of either team.

FORCED SHOT: a hurried shot taken by a player who is being closely guarded and does not take his normal time to shoot.

FOULED OUT: being required to leave the game after committing five fouls.

FOUL LINE: free throw line.

FOUL TROUBLE: a player has to leave the court when he has accumulated five fouls; when four or five members of your team are 'fouled out' your team is in trouble.

FORWARD: the name of one of the positions in the team. The forwards play on offence in the area of court on either the right- or left-hand side, between the restricted area and the side lines.

FREE BALL (loose ball): a ball which, although in play, is not in the possession of either team.

FREELANCE PLAY: a term applied to play where the team has no set offensive system, the various members of the team moving the ball as they wish.

FREEZING THE BALL (stalling): the action of a team in possession of the ball who attempt to retain possession of the ball without an attempt to score. Limited to 30 seconds and often used late in the game in an effort to protect a slight lead.

FRONT COURT: that half of the court that contains the basket which a team is attacking.

FRONTING THE POST: guarding the post-player in front rather than between him and the basket. A defensive tactic aiming to prevent a good post-player from receiving the ball close to the basket.

FRONT SCREEN: a screen set up by an offensive player between a team-mate and the team-mate's opponent.

FULL-COURT PRESS: a pressing defence which operates throughout the whole court and not merely in the defender's back court (see *press*).

FUNDAMENTALS: the basic skills of the game, necessary as a background for all team play.

GIVE AND GO: an offensive manoeuvre in which a

player passes the ball to a team-mate and cuts towards basket for a return pass.

GUARD (playmaker): the name of one of the positions on the team, usually played by the shorter players, who on offence will play in the area of court between the centre line and the free-throw line (extended to the side-lines).

GUNNER: a player who shoots more often than he should and who rarely passes to a team-mate.

HALF-COURT PRESS: a pressing defence which operates in a team's back court.

HAND-OFF: passing the ball quickly to a team-mate moving with or toward you. This is a short pass, not more than one metre.

HANDS-UP DEFENCE: defensive players keeping their hands up to make shots and passes more difficult.

HIGH: a position played by an offensive player who plays in the area of court away from the end line near to the free throw line.

HOOP: the basket.

INSIDE:
- ☐ in the under basket area;
- ☐ between the perimeter of the defence and the basket they are defending;
- ☐ 'inside' the key.

JAM-UP: when a defensive team clogs the middle of the court.

JUMP-BALL: a jump-ball takes place when the official tosses the ball between two opposing players.

KEY (keyhole): the restricted area including the circle, derived from the original keyhole shape.

LANE: see *restricted area*.

LEAD PASS: a pass thrown ahead of the intended receiver so that he can catch the ball on the move and maintain his speed.

LOW: a position held by an offensive player operating in the area of court near to the end line or basket.

MAN-TO-MAN DEFENCE: a style of defence where each player is assigned to guard a specific opponent.

MIS-MATCH: if you and your opponent are equally tall and your team-mate and his opponent are each taller, you would be at a considerable disadvantage if you switched as a result of a pick or screen; and this would be a mis-match.

OFFENSIVE BOARD: the backboard that a team is attacking.

OUT-OF-BOUNDS: the area outside the legal playing court; i.e., outside the inside edge of the lines marking the side-lines and the end-lines.

ONE-ON-ONE (lvl): the situation where one offensive

player attacks one defensive player.

OPTIONS: alternative offensive manoeuvres than can occur during a game.

OUTLET PASS: the first pass made after a defensive rebound, usually made to a player stationed near to the closest sideline of the court and used to initiate a fast break.

OUTSIDE:
- nearer the sideline of the court than the basket;
- between the sideline and the perimeter of the defence;
- 'outside' the key.

OVERLOAD: outnumber.

OVERTIME: the extra period(s) played after the expiration of the second half of a game in which the score has been tied.

PALMING THE BALL: a violation occurring when a player turns his wrist and hand as he dribbles, enabling him to protect and control the ball between bounces.

PASS AND CUT: see *give and go*.

PATTERN: the predetermined positional formation adopted by an offensive team prior to their initiating offensive manoeuvres. Common patterns are 1:3:1 and 2:3.

PATTERN PLAY: offensive plays initiated from fixed and predetermined court positions.

PICK (side screen): a screen set at the side of a team-mate's opponent.

PICK AND ROLL: a pick followed by a pivot towards the basket by the player who has set the screen, useful against a switching man-to-man defence.

PIVOT PLAYER: another name for a *post-player* (q.v.).

PLAYMAKER: a player who is adept at setting up situations that will enable team-mates to have a scoring opportunity. (see also *guard*.)

PLAY: a term used to describe a series of movements of players and/or the ball on court, mainly used for offensive manoeuvres.

POSSESSION: control of the ball.

POST:
- see *post-player*;
- an offensive manoeuvre in which a player takes up a position usually with his back to the basket he is attacking, thus providing a target to receive a pass and/or act as a rear screen to enable team-mates to run their opponents into the post.

POST-PLAYER: usually the tallest player in the team, who operates on offence in an area near the sides of, and occasionally in, the free-throw lane and close to the basket. He is stationed there for scoring purposes and to feed cutters, and is a player around whom the offensive team pivot. He is therefore sometimes called a pivot player.

PRESS: a defensive attempt to force the opposing team into making some kind of error and thus lose possession of the ball. It is accomplished usually by aggressive defence, double-teaming or harrassing the ballhandler with attempts to tie up the ball. The press can be applied full court, half court or any other fractional part of the playing area and can be based on either man-to-man or zone principles.

REBOUND: a term used to describe the actual retrieving of the ball as it rebounds from the backboard or the ring after an unsuccessful shot. *Offensive rebound* therefore means gaining the rebound from the team's offensive basket (i.e., the one it is attacking). *Defensive rebound* is retrieving the ball from the team's defensive basket (i.e., the basket they are defending).

REBOUND TRIANGLE: a term used to describe the positioning of a group of three defenders who form a triangle around the basket after a shot has been attempted. This is to cover the probable positions of the ball should a rebound occur and to prevent an opponent from gaining a good position from which to collect the rebound.

REVERSE (roll): a change of direction in which the offensive player endeavours to free himself from a close marking defender. The change of direction is executed after a move towards the defender and a pivot so that the offensive player turns his back on his opponent and then moves off in the new direction.

SAFETY MAN: an offensive player who plays in the guard position with the aim of defending against possible fast breaks on loss of possession, and to receive a pass when an offensive play breaks down.

SAG: when a defender moves away from his opponent towards the basket he is defending.

SAGGING DEFENCE: a team defensive tactic in which the defenders furthest from the ball sag away from their opponents towards the basket to help their team-mates and cover the high-percentage scoring area.

SCREEN: a screen occurs when an offensive player attempts to prevent a defender from reaching a desired position or maintaining his defensive position. The screen is intended to impede the progress of the defender so that the offensive player he is marking has an unimpeded shot or a clear path to basket.

SCRIMMAGE: a practice game, usually without any officials.

SERIES: a name given to a number of plays used by

an offensive team in particular situations; e.g., high post plays.

SET PLAY:
- a repetitive pre-arranged form of offence;
- a play executed to pre-determined and rehearsed moves which, when applied in certain set situations in the game, is intended to result in a favourable scoring chance. The set situations are usually out-of-bounds, jump-ball or at a free-throw.

SET-UP: the action of establishing an offensive pattern or the defensive organisation.

SLIDE: when a defensive player, in order to prevent himself from being screened, moves, as he follows his own opponent, between a team-mate and that team-mate's opponent.

SLOW BREAK: a deliberate attack against a defence that is set-up.

STALLING: see *freezing the ball*.

STEAL: to take the ball away from an opponent (or intercept).

STRONG SIDE: refers to the side of the court on which the offensive team has the ball at any particular time.

SWITCH: a defensive manoeuvre in which two defenders exchange defensive responsibilities by changing the men they are guarding. It occurs usually during a screen situation in which one of the defenders can no longer guard his man because of the screen.

SYSTEM: a team's basic offensive and defensive plays.

THREE-POINT PLAY: when a player is fouled in the act of shooting, but scores, he has the opportunity to convert one free throw and so gain a third point.

TIE-UP: a defensive situation in which the defenders through their defensive tactics gain a held ball.

TIP: the momentary catching and pushing of the ball towards the basket, executed by an offensive rebounder in an attempt to score from an offensive rebound while he is still in the air.

TIP-OFF: the centre jump-ball at the start of play.

TRAILER: an offensive player who follows behind the ball-handler.

TRAP: a 'double team' in which two defenders attempt to stop a dribbler and prevent him from making a successful pass.

TRANSPOSITION: this occurs after the change of possession as a team moves from offence to defence and *vice versa*.

TURNOVER: the loss of ball-possession without there

having been an attempt by the offensive team to shoot at basket.

TWO FROM THREE: when a player is fouled in the act of shooting but fails to make the basket he is given three shots from which to make two. (Thus if his first two shots are successful he does not take the third.)

WEAK SIDE: the opposite side of the court to the *strong side* (q.v.).

ZONE DEFENCE: a team's defensive tactic in which the five defensive players react to the ball and in so doing are each responsible for an area of the court in which they move in relation to the movements of the ball.

Appendix

DETAILS OF THE LEAGUES AND CUP COMPETITIONS WITHIN BRITAIN; NAMES AND ADDRESSES OF NATIONAL LEAGUE CLUBS, AREAS AND AREA SECRETARIES

English Basketball Association (EBBA)

Administrator M. D. Welch
Administrative Offices Calomax House, Lupton Avenue, Leeds 9.
The EBBA (which includes the Channel Islands) is divided into about thirty Area Associations and ten National Associations. These associations together control the basketball activities in England; and in some instances the National Associations, also controlling relevant activities in Scotland and Wales as well (for example, the armed forces, civil service, universities and paraplegics). Details of these forty associations, secretaries' names and addresses are provided in the current basketball yearbook, available from M. D. Welch.

English basketball is organised at national, regional and local levels as follows:

National level
- men's national league with two divisions and totalling 21 clubs;
- women's national league with two divisions (these leagues are actually composed of both English and Scottish clubs at the moment but in future years may be restricted to English clubs) and totalling 15 clubs.

Regional level
- five men's leagues covering the whole of England;

101

- two women's leagues covering the east and southeast of England.

Local level
- an extensive network totalling some 70 men's and 10 women's leagues registered with the appropriate area association;
- approximately 75 schools associations, similarly registered, and which control the leagues and other basketball competitions within schools.

In addition, the EBBA promotes and controls national knock-out cup competitions for men and women at junior, intermediate and senior level. These competitions are supplemented throughout the season by leagues arranging their own cup competitions and by individual clubs promoting both their own cup competitions and their own tournaments with other clubs, drawn from international, national and/or local level.

Amateur Basketball Association of Scotland (ABAS)

Administrator K. D. A. Johnston
Association Offices 8 Frederick Street, Edinburgh EH2 2HB

The ABAS is divided into seven Regional Associations and a Schools Basketball Association. These associations control the basketball activities in Scotland together with the National Associations referred to under the section on the EBBA. Details of these ABAS associations and secretaries' names and addresses are available from the association offices.

Scottish Basketball is also organised at national, regional and local level as follows:

National level
- men's national league with two leagues and totalling 20 clubs;
- women's national league with one division and some 6 clubs.

(it is possible that the EBBA women's national league, referred to earlier, will in future years be only for English clubs. Currently, the ABAS National league is also open to English clubs.)

Regional and local level

The seven Regional Associations control both regional and local basketball and there are about 25 men's leagues and 10 women's leagues covering the whole of Scotland.

The Schools Basketball Association is formed on the same regional basis as described above with some 180 registered schools; it provides an extensive network of leagues throughout the country and a national knock-out cup for the under 14s through to the under 17s and then on an open basis for both boys and girls.

Similarly, the ABAS promotes and controls national knock-out cup competitions for men and women at youth, junior and senior level. These competitions, as elsewhere, are supplemented during each season by Regional Associations and leagues arranging their own cup competitions, and by individual clubs promoting their own tournaments.

Welsh Amateur Basketball Association (WABA)

Honorary General Secretary I. G. Jones
Address 5 Manor Drive, Coychurch, Bridgend, Glam. Details of secretaries' names and addresses can be obtained from the Honorary General Secretary. Welsh basketball is organised at national, regional and local levels as follows.

National level
- men's national league with one division which is currently limited to eight teams.

Regional level
- five men's leagues with about 60 teams covering North, Central and South Wales;
- one women's league with 11 teams based in South Wales.

Local level

The details of the men's and women's leagues can be obtained from I. G. Jones. Features include two leagues of mini-basketball in Glamorgan for boys and girls with 18 teams taking part.

The Welsh Schools Association has almost 80 schools or junior clubs registered with it and organises leagues and competitions for boys from under 14 right through to under 19 and for girls at the under 15 and under 19 levels only.

These competitions are supplemented by knock-out cup competitions for men and women at national level and a league winners' cup for regional and national league winners.

National League Clubs and Home Court

Division One (Men)
A.T.S. Giants, Sale Leisure Centre.
Bowmer & Kirkland A.S., Loughborough College of Education.
Cinzano S.C.P., Crystal Palace National Sports Centre.
Embassy M.K., Milton Keynes Leisure Centre.
London Y.M.C.A. Metros, London Central Y.M.C.A.
St Lukes T.S.B., Exeter College.
Stockport Belgrade, Peel Moat Sports Centre, Stockport.
Team Fiat, Coventry Sports Centre.
Vauxhall Motors, Bunyan Centre, Bedford.
Wilson Panthers, Adwick Leisure Centre, Doncaster.

Division Two (Men)
Avenue, Picketts Lock Sports Centre, Edmonton.
Birmingham Bulldogs, Haden Hill Leisure Centre.
Bromley, Walnuts Sports Centre, Orpington.
Derby C.F.E., Derby College of F.E.

Epab, Sunderland Sports Centre.
Hemel Hempstead Lakers, Dacorum Sports Centre, Hemel Hempstead.
K.C.A. Telefusion, Warbreck School, Blackpool.
Leatherhead, Leatherhead Sports Centre.
Miles Mustangs, Scatcherd Sports Centre, Morley.
Nottingham, Nottingham University S.C.
Seensee Sonics, Maidenhead Sports Centre.

Division One (Women)
Cleveland Eagles, Norton School, Stockton-on-Tees.
Corvus Cornix, Kerridge Sports Hall, Cambridge.
Griffins, Paternoster Sports Centre, Waltham Abbey.
London Y.M.C.A. Bobcats, London Central Y.M.C.A.
Norwich Coe-Stars, University of East Anglia.
Radcliffe Wildcats, Dayncourt School, Radcliffe-on-Trent.
Southgate T.C. Wisps, Arnos School, Southgate.
Tigers, Dacorum Sports Centre, Hemel Hempstead.

Division Two (Women)
Avon Wanderers, Whitchurch Sports Centre, Bristol.
Chantry Bobcats, Chantry School, Ipswich.
Liverpool Ajax, Norton Recreation Centre, Runcorn.

Malory, Crofton Leisure Centre, Lewisham.
Sheffield Hatters, Earl Marshall Campus, Sheffield.
Solent Shrimps, Redbridge Sports Centre, Southampton.

Area Associations (Secretaries)

Bedfordshire and Cambridgeshire: Mr B. W. Head, 51 Austin Road, Luton, Beds.
Buckinghamshire and Oxfordshire: Mr A. E. Bridge, 13 Alexandra Road, Botley, Oxford OX2 0DD.
Cleveland: T. C. Moore, 39 Armadale Close, Bishopton Road West, Stockton, Cleveland.
Derbyshire and Nottinghamshire: T. Hooper, Hopwell High School, Oakbrook, Derby.
Durham: C. Donaghy, 31 Campbell Street, Tow Law, Bishop Auckland, Co. Durham.
Essex: J. Lloyd, 'Ellwood', Coach Road, Great Horkesley, Colchester, Essex.
Gloucestershire: J. Llewelyn, 140 Hatherley Road, Cheltenham, Gloucestershire.
Greater Manchester and N.E. Cheshire: D. W. McLean, 20 Berwick Avenue, Heaton Mersey, Stockport, Cheshire.
Guernsey: E. D. McDonaugh, Myrtle Place, Port Soif Lane, Vale, Guernsey.
Hertfordshire: D. Moon, 46 Longcroft Road, Maple Cross, Rickmansworth, Herts.
Isle of Man: Mr P. G. Deadman, M.B.E., 19 Mill Street, Castletown, Isle of Man.
Jersey: Mr T. Jehan, La Franchise, St. Martini Jersey.
Kent: Lyn Marsh, 86 Northdown Road, Welling, Kent DA16 1NA.
Leicestershire: K. Youles, 63 Lower Packington Road, Ashby-De-La-Zouch, Leicester LE6 5QD.
Lincolnshire and South Humberside: M. Andrews, 2 Church View Crescent, Fiskerton, Lincoln, Lincs.
London: Mr P. J. Horn, 26 Ickenham Close, Ruislip, Middlesex.
Merseyside and N.W. Cheshire: R. Holm, 10 Eilian Avenue, Liverpool 14.
Norfolk: D. Goodley, High Copse, Halvergate, Norfolk NR17 1PL.
Northamptonshire: P. K. Mattli, 67 Roche Way, Wellingborough, Northants.
North East: A. Ralph, 59 Newlyn Drive, Parkside Dale, Cramlington, Northumberland.
North Staffordshire and South Cheshire: Mr R. C.

Lovell, 45 Grange Road, Cheddleton, Near Leek, ST13 7HU.

North West: G. Emmett, 31 Coniston Avenue, Cleveleys, Blackpool.

Solent: P. Smith, Hope Cottage, Magdala Road, Hayling Island, Hants.

South West: R. D. Wooldridge, 112 Roselands Drive, Paignton, Devon.

Suffolk: D. Jackaman, 198 Colchester Road, Ipswich.

Surrey: G. H. Cole, 10 Royal Hill Court, Greenwich High Road, London, S.E.10.

Sussex: P. Bowles, 85 Overdown Rise, Portslade, Sussex.

Warwickshire: Mrs L. Shaw, 68 Daventry Road, Coventry.

Wessex: Mrs M. A. Ball, 11 Chaffinch Close, Kempshot, Basingstoke, Hants.

West: Mr R. Gallop, 95 Cloverlea Road, Oldland Common, Bristol.

West Midlands: Mr K. Mumford 262 Rectory Road, Sutton Coldfield, Warks.

Wiltshire: D. V. Watkins, 14 Laburnum Drive, Wootton Bassett, Wilts.

Yorkshire and North Humberside: Dr F. Spode, 52 Carterknowle Avenue, Sheffield S11 9FU.

Index

Index

administrators, 11
air dribble, 91
alive, 91
arc, 91
areas of responsibility, 16
attacking the gaps, 65, 66

backboard, 52, 91
back court, 25, 91
backdoor, 91
back-in, 91
back-tap, 91
ball control game, 91
ball-handler, 58, 60, 63
ball hawk, 91
ball-hog, 40
bank shot, 92
baseline drive, 92
bell/buzzer 14
benches, 14

blocking out, 92
box and one, 92
break, 92; *see* fast-break
brush-off, 92
buttonhook, 92

centre, 24, 63, 92
centre circle, 19, 25
charging, 92
chaser, 92
check, 92
club secretary/treasurer, 12
clubs, 11
circulation, 92
clear out, 92
clear the boards, 92
clutch shooter, 92
coaches, 14, 15
combination defence, 92
competitions, 11
contact, 92
continuity play, 92
control basketball, 93
controlling the boards, 93
corner man, 93
cross-court pass, 93
crossover, 93
court layout, 12
cut, 93
cutaway, 93
cutter, 93
cutting drills, 78

dead, 93
defence, 7, 52
defending, 7, 28
defensive board, 93
disqualifying foul, 27
double foul, 26
double screens, 93
double team, 93
dribbling, 7, 19, 35, 40; low dribble, 40; high dribble, 40
drill, 93
drive, 93
dunk, 93

equipment, 9

fake, 29, 43, 93
fall-away, 93
fast-break, 93
Fédération Internationale de Basketball Amateur, 7
feed, 94
fees, 12
feint, 93; *see* fake
field goal, 26
first receiver, 47,
five fouls, 27
five-second rule, 24, 62
fixtures, 12,
floating, 94
floor-play, 94
follow the leader, 70
forced shot, 94
fouled out, 94
foul line, 94

foul trouble, 94
fouls, 14, 23, 25, 26, 27, 55
forward, 94
free ball, 94
free shot, 25, 37
free throw, 25
free throw lines, 24
freelance play, 94
freezing the ball, 94
front court, 25, 94
fronting the post, 94
front screen, 94
full-court press, 94
fundamentals, 94

game clock, 14
give and go, 95
guard, 20, 63, 95
gunner, 95

half-court press, 95
hand-off, 95
hands-up defence, 95
high, 95
hoop, 95

individual defence, 43
individual skills, 28, 72
inside, 95

jam-up, 95
jump-ball, 19, 25, 95
jump shots, 34

junior players, 11

key (keyhole), 53, 95
key way, 7, 19, 68
kit, 9

lane, 95
lay-up, 34, 35
lead pass, 95
leagues, 11
local basketball association, 11, 101
local league secretary, 11

man-to-man defence, 52, 57, 68, 95
match ball, 12
mini-basketball, 80
mis-match, 95
multiple foul, 26

Naismith, Dr James, 7
National Association Affiliation Fee, 12, 101
National Schools Association, 11, 101
New York, 9
numbers, 15

offence, 7; 1-2-2 Offence, 68
offensive board, 95
officials, 16
One-on-one (1v1), 70, 95
options, 96
out-of-bounds, 95
outlet pass, 96
outside, 96

overload, 66, 96
overtime, 96

palming the ball, 95
pass and cut, 95
passing the ball, 28, 29, 31
passing drills, 76
passive defence, 73
pattern, 96
patterns of defence, 52
pattern play, 96
pepperpot, 76
personal fouls, 23, 25
pick, 96
pick and roll, 96
pivoting, 19
playing times, 24
playmaker, 63, 96
play, 96
players, 15
playing regulations, 24
points, 19
possession, 96
post, 50, 96
post player, 45, 50, 63, 96
practice balls, 12
press, 52, 61, 97
pressure defence, 52, 57, 59; *see* press

rebound, 26, 97
rebound triangle, 96
receiving the ball, 28, 33
referee, 16

111

reverse, 97
rules, 7, 15

safety man, 97
sag, 57
sagging defence, 97
school, 9, 11
score-book, 14, 16
scorer, 16
scoring, 19, 28
screen, 20, 55, 68, 69, 97
scrimmage game, 72, 97
second receiver, 45, 47
senior players, 11
series, 97
set play, 98
set shot, 37
set-up, 98
shooting,
shooting, 28, 34, 37; lay-up, 34, 35, 73; jump shot, 34, 74; free shot, foul shot, 37
shooting drills, 73
slide, 98
slow break, 98
split the post, 78
stall, 98
stance, 37, 45, 50
steal, 55, 58, 98
strong side, 98
substitutes, 14, 15, 27
switch, 56, 98
system, 98

team defence, 52, 72
team practice, 70
technical foul, 25
ten fouls by a team, 27
thirty-second operator, 14, 16
thirty-second rule, 19, 25
thirty-second clock (or watch), 14
three-point play, 98
three-second area, 19, 52; *see* keyway
tie, 24
tie-up, 98
timekeeper, 14, 16
tip, 98
tip-off, 98
trailer, 98
trap, 98
transposition, 98
turnover, 98
two from three, 98

umpire, 16
USA, 9

weak side, 98

YMCA, 9
YWCA, 9

Zone defence, 52, 53, 65, 98